ב"ה

# Where the Woods meet the Water

by

## Gila Margolin

*Towards Holy Week 2016*

*To Alston –
Well met in UC!
In Peace & Friendship
Shalom
שלום*

*Gila*

GW00500685

Published by

*The Little Sisters of Joy*

Published by

THE LITTLE SISTERS OF JOY

The Haven, 61 Edgecombe, Cambridge CB4 2 LW, England, UK

© THE LITTLE SISTERS OF JOY 2014

Printed in England by
Victoire Press
1 Trafalgar way, Bar Hill
Cambridge, CB23 8SQ

Trade Paperback: ISBN 0-9553007- 1-1
also 13 digit no.: ISBN 978-0-9553007-1-4

Front Cover: From an original painting by Anna Bristow.
The painting is an illustration of the Laurentian Shield.

For
Dr Nigel Hymas
for his
wisdom and understanding

and
for
Canada
my spiritual home

Ich lebe mein Leben in wachsenden Ringen,
die sich uber die Dinge ziehen.
Ich werde den letzten vielleicht nicht vollbringen,
aber versuchen will ich ihn.
Ich kreise um Gott, um den uralten Turm,
und ich kreise jahrtausendelang;
und ich weiss noch nicht: bin ich ein Falke, ein Sturm
oder ein grosser Gesang.


I live my life in increasing circles,
which extend themselves over all.
Perhaps I will not complete the last one,
but try I certainly will.


I circle round God, round the age-old tower,
and I circle a thousand years long;
and I don't know yet: whether I am a falcon, a storm
or a Great Song.


Rainer Maria Rilke
(from *Das Stundenbuch*)

# Acknowledgements

To Maryvonne le Goanvic, who helped me to give birth to
*The Little Sisters of Joy*

To James Kinnier Wilson, a kindred spirit, for his love and support

To Michael Loewe, a dear friend, who thought I had a second book in me

To all at the Regent Hotel, Cambridge UK, for their tender loving care

To Jeff Houghton, for his wholehearted friendship and encouragement

To Sofian from Provence, where this book starts

To the Cambridge City Hotel, for providing the space to write

To Marta, for her solidarity

To Liesel, for her clarity and compassion

3

## Prelude

Like my last autobiographical book, *The Moving Swan*, this little book has been six years in the making. It describes my life between 1999 and 2009 and my love affair, set to last a lifetime, with Canada and particularly Toronto, which I regard as my spiritual home.

Most people think that 'Toronto' means 'Meeting Place' but, according to a lady I met in the Native Canadian (First Nations) Centre in Toronto in June 2013, Toronto means 'Where the woods meet the water', hence the title of this book.

I cannot track down the native language from which the word 'Toronto' comes, but the Algonquin tribe bring people together in the *Kumik*, a traditional meeting place, where First Nation elders share their wisdom with members of the First Nations and non-members alike. The *Kumik* provides a unique place where young or old can sit and talk, share their concerns and learn to appreciate their respective cultures.

I like to think that this special place is *'where the woods meet the water'*.

Gila Margolin, Cambridge, UK, December 2013

Gila Margolin, in Native Canadian Centre, Toronto

# What came before

## (A brief synopsis of my life, as in *The Moving Swan*, Part I of my memoirs)

I was born into an Orthodox Jewish family in London in 1951. I went to a Jewish primary school and learned to love the Synagogue, Sabbath and festivals. When I was eleven, we moved to Glasgow, which was a watershed in many senses. I was exposed to my first Christian influences and, in acting in my school play, *A Man for All Seasons*, came to know and love the great Christian Saint, Thomas More.

At sixteen, I had already left home and one night had a dream about Jesus. My friend took me to a lady in the Presbyterian church in the hope I would discover more but I was entering my wild youth, a period, during the late 60s, of turbulence and amorality. The highlights of that time were my study of the German language at Glasgow University and singing with my guitar, which was to prove such a seminal pursuit in later years.

A massive breakdown ensued, which proved to be cathartic and culminated in my coming back to God through singing. When I went up the stairs to the teacher's flat in Glasgow and he greeted me, it was as if a huge door opened in my heart. I had found a companion, Robin, who lived in Edinburgh and I would spend happy weekends there.

But for all the human solidarity in Glasgow, my heart was yearning for pastures new and, in 1982, I moved with all my belongings to Cambridge, where I knew no one but where I had been granted a place on a Foundation Music Course at what was then fondly known as 'the Tech'.

My piano teacher knew of my ambitions to become a singer

and she soon teamed me up with a wonderful pianist, David, who became my husband as well as my playing partner. He encouraged me to find a Jewish community; the Reform group asked me to help them with their services and soon my faith deepened and I needed to reflect.

A week's stay at St Beuno's Retreat Centre in North Wales was an unforeseen life-changing experience. As a result of this and many other mystical experiences, and a reading of the New Testament, I decided to become a Catholic. Just to make sure, I went to Eastern Canada at the invitation of a friend in June 1988 and it was there, amidst the overwhelming presence of God among the pine trees of the Canadian Shield (one of the oldest rock formations in the world), that I made my decision. To confirm it still further, an angel/messenger told me to go to the Shrine of Sainte Anne de Beaupré, situated along the St. Lawrence River in Quebec, where I asked for the intercession of the Virgin Mary in my life and felt I got a response.

I was received into the Catholic Church on 25 March 1989. I had already embarked on a Hebrew degree at Lucy Cavendish College in the University of Cambridge. Over the years I started using my gifts by teaching Hebrew to a variety of individuals and giving little Hebrew Fun Days. I was given to realise from the outset of my conversion that everything I had learned from life as a practising Jewess could be used for God's work in my new life; indeed, it was a wonderful formation. I went to Israel in 1989 to study Hebrew in a summer programme at the Hebrew University, and made some new Arab friends. In 1990 I studied Arabic there. I had already been feeling that I had a vocation to become a nun and early in 1998 a Jesuit friend said to me, 'You definitely have a vocation, but you are not young, so either become a member of an already established group, or start a community of your own.'    *And this is what comes next...*

**1 February 1999**

**Cambridge, UK**

Last night I dreamt that I was in Pomeyrol again. The moon was full, with its complete corona, deep and mysterious, hanging over the *maison de silence*, and the stars were copious in the night sky. I felt that I was the only one in the world.

In the Indian tradition, when you see the moon like this it is either a sign of a death or a miracle. The call I had experienced in December 1998 to found a community was definitely a miracle.

**7 March 1999**

Our community is born. Maryvonne and I have called it *The Little Sisters of Joy*, after the Little Sisters of Jesus and because we have an admiration for St Francis and his love of poverty and joy. It is fitting that we met today in Benigna's house at Newton Road, Cambridge, for the first time, through a friend. Although I was still exhausted from my trip in December and January and from everything else that has been going on, Maryvonne insisted that I tell her everything of these last events as it is important. It is to be a community of *Prayer* and *Praise* and *Peace*.

Maryvonne is going to Israel, where she is taking a Hebrew course, and I hope one day to join her in community there.

**14 August 1999**

Today I went to see my Bishop near Norwich. Peter Smith picked me up from the station and drove me down to Poringland, where the Bishop of East Anglia resides. We chatted in the garden over drinks and somewhere in the conversation he said it was *providential* that we were meeting today because normally his diary is so full and he can't see people for months. I felt very honoured. David had suggested I tell the Bishop about my experience in Israel, on the kibbutz, where I had been from April to June ... how I had felt a reconciling of opposites within myself. The Bishop listened carefully, especially when I said, yes, I knew it was early days, but that I felt God was calling me to found a new religious community within the Church.

He gave me a very pleasant lunch and put me at my ease, chatting about his nice neighbours. Finally he said he would drive me back to the station in Norwich.

As he gently ushered me into the car, he said, almost casually, 'Well, if you write a Rule of Life, I suppose I will have to authorise it...'

I hardly dared to draw breath as I took in this momentous statement.

## 15 August 1999, Feast of the Assumption

I woke up this morning and the Holy Spirit has inspired me to start writing the Rule of Life. I have covered eight main sections so far: *Prayer, Community Living, Dress, Hospitality, Love and Reconciliation, Days of Retreat, Vows and Fraternities* (this last being very much in the spirit of The Little Sisters of Jesus). I seem to be drawing on much of my Jewish background, especially when it comes to the sharing of meals (like a sacrament), keeping a day of rest (a Shabbat), and hospitality, which, although I have only mentioned the Book of Hebrews, actually goes back to Abraham and the Angels, when he entertained them in the heat of the day.

But I am integrating the Rule with my Christianity and my love of Jesus particularly. I think structures are important but I want the whole thing to be fun as well so my sense of humour seems to be shining through. I have Rabbi Blue's eleventh commandment for when we get too tired from looking after people:

*Thou shalt not make thyself a doormat!*

I think the most important section so far is on *Love and Reconciliation*, so I have written: '*Strive to do all for the love of God alone. Use your gifts, including your musical and artistic ones, for the glory of God and to effect peace, healing and reconciliation with your fellow man. Trust and be at peace with one another.*' This is a quotation from St Peter; actually, I have peppered this section with quotes from his letters as I am so fond of him.

The Vows are the stickiest of all; I will have to get help but at least I am having a go. And I am sure that Our Lady, whose special day it is today, is helping me.

**Later that day in the 'upper room' at Newton Road**

David was passing and 'happened' to pop in. I told him what was going on and he was thrilled. He glanced at my writings and said, '*Well done, but now write a commentary!*'

So I have attempted a few pages based on the sections I have already written.

The whole thing is only six pages long, but I think it is succinct and clear. I intend to send a copy to Maryvonne in Israel. And of course to the Bishop, once it's a little more refined.

**20 September 1999**

One of the most important things that the Bishop said to me was that it is not always easy to discern God's will. Today was a dark day. I received a card from Maryvonne in Israel saying that she had read the Rule of Life, but that she could no longer continue 'walking my way'. She asked me to forgive her, in keeping with the Liturgy, as she had deliberately chosen to write on Yom Kippur, (the 11th September this year), the most solemn day in the Jewish calendar, when the people ask for forgiveness from God and each other.

There were differences in opinion about the dress code (I initially put forward a rather radical suggestion) but apart from this I thought the Rule was, in its own way, quite Orthodox. I have the uneasy feeling that there is more to this than meets the eye and I think the only way to resolve it is to return to Israel and meet Maryvonne face to face. But of course I can't do it now, so it will have to wait till the beginning of next year, especially since I left Israel under a cloud this year.

All I can think of right now is what Sister Madeleine, Founder of The Little Sisters of Jesus, used to say:

*He took me by the hand and, blindly, I followed.*

**4 October 1999**

I think I have just made a new friend. She has just applied to do care work and I was showing her the ropes. We were in Mrs Alphonse's house, so, as is the custom in Singapore, we had to take our shoes off. Mrs Alphonse was pleased that there were two of us to help her get ready for the day. Anyhow, I asked Clare what she been doing recently and she told me that she had just got back from three months in Israel! This made for an instant bond, as I had spent three months this spring in Israel myself. Clare is tall, friendly, with a very open face. About 24 years old.

She also asked me where I went to church and I told her that I went to OLEM (Our Lady and the English Martyrs), the big Catholic Church on Hills Road. She wants to come with me on Sunday.

## 11 December 1999

Clare was received into the Church last week; it was very fast, but she has studied Theology and feels she already knows something about the religion from me, which is very flattering. I am beginning to feel very close to her and even having maternal feelings towards her ... that's a first for me. I asked Renata in London what I should do and she said I have to tell her.

## 14 December 1999

I cooked a nice dinner and invited Clare round. We were upstairs and I was behind the little glass sliding window, doing the cooking. Clare was on the other side. '*I have something to tell you*,' I said. 'I have been having all these maternal feelings towards you.' '*So, you have a daughter*,' said Clare, as she lifted her arms, and I knew that everything would be okay.

## 16 December 1999

Today I am feeling a bit blue. I had difficulties with a client and have lost my job. I will go and see Father Brendan to see if he can offer any wise advice.

**18 December 1999**

I went to see Fr Brendan at our usual appointed hour of ten at night on a Saturday. He works so hard, poor man, and I am sure he only sleeps for a few hours. He is completely dedicated to what he does, in the University as a history Don and as the priest for Lady Margaret House, where the nuns live. Anyhow, I crossed the Mathematical Bridge in Queens' College and found the courtyard where his rooms are. Sometimes I knock and he asks me to wait for a few minutes while he finishes with someone.

Once inside, I feel completely calm and he always gives me good advice. This time I was complaining that I had lost my job. And was also having the feeling that I was going to die. Father Brendan listened, then said I was a mystic and he was sorry, but St John the Evangelist, the greatest mystic, also had those feelings of longing to be with God. He had to wait and was confined to living on Mount Athos for the rest of his natural life.

As for the job, he simply said, '*God will find you a new work.*'

**25 December 1999**

It has been the most extraordinary Christmas ever. Several things seem to be happening all at once. Yesterday, Christmas Eve, I said to Benigna that as we were on our own we could have a nice quiet time listening to the Nine Lessons and Carols from King's. She came upstairs to my living room (which I still think of as the Upper Room) and we listened attentively and chatted in between. She offered me a nice supper and wondered if I would like to accompany her to the midnight service in Trumpington Parish Church, where she goes quite regularly. I said I would be very happy to do so.

It was moving to see an old lady get down on her knees in the rather confined pew and, as I knelt beside her, I thought how close I felt to her. After all, she was virtually the first person I met in Cambridge, on that famous night when I came to her home for a choir rehearsal in the first week I arrived in Cambridge in August 1982.

The service was lovely, with a great sense of holiness, and I think we both went to bed with a feeling of joy.

Fardijah, Benigna's daughter, and Maryam, her granddaughter, arrived the next day with Latif, her son-in-law, who had not been at all well, but who was looking quite splendid in his dressing gown and who ate a hearty Christmas meal. Latif is such a wonderful composer, especially with his settings of Tagore. Benigna had worried that the milkman wouldn't deliver the pudding on time, but it came. We drank a '*LeChayim*' and then suddenly I looked at Latif and just knew that he wasn't well. Fardijah bundled him into the car to take him to the hospital but he died peacefully on the way.

I went upstairs when I heard and lit a large candle and felt a sense of awe and wonder.

**27 December 1999**

There is no doubt that death and birth are interconnected. Shortly after Latif died, we had a brief visit from David to say that Rebecca was in labour and that they were going to '*have a puppy*'. I was entertaining a young man and his friend upstairs the next day when I offered them some tea and cakes and said a blessing in Hebrew. At this point, all the plates in the cupboard came out with a loud bang (but not broken) and the young man said, '*That was a powerful blessing!*' Then the phone rang and it was David to say that they had had a baby boy.

**30 December 1999**

My father-in-law, Paul Christophersen, lived just long enough to see a photo of his only grandson, named Paul after him. Paul senior died this morning, after a short illness and a long career as a professor of English Language, distinguished in his native country of Denmark as well as in Norway, Ireland, the Middle East and the UK. Long before David and I met, Paul vied for the Chair of English Language at Glasgow University, which cousin Michael Samuels actually got. Paul and Michael, and their wives Peggy and Hilary, were great friends.

What I remember best about Paul was his goodness and courtesy and the fact that although he thought David was too young to marry, he was happy that he was going to have a Jewish wife. He himself had had a Jewish fiancée before he married Peggy.

My parents-in-law took me on a family holiday to Denmark in 1986 and I could see from that holiday how much Paul, the gentle academic, sometimes stern father, was loved. I will miss him.

**22 January 2000, Cambridge**

**Jewish New Year for Trees**

Sometime over the past year, I had a dream. I dreamt that Cardinal Lustiger, whom I had visited in January 1999, told me, quite clearly, that I must celebrate the birthday of *The Little Sisters of Joy* on Tu Bishvat, the Jewish New Year for Trees. What better day could there be! It's a movable feast which I loved in my childhood. As a pupil in my Jewish primary school in Golders Green, we were asked to come on this day with as many different kinds of fruits as possible, some quite exotic in those days!

Today, in the afternoon, a group of about ten of us gathered in Benigna's large garden for the planting of our first silver birch tree. The gardener had already made a large hole in preparation for the little tree to go into the ground. The other day, Benigna and I drove out especially to a tree nursery in Fordham, near Newmarket, where we picked this lovely little tree.

As we gathered in the garden, we recited together Psalm 96:

*Let the heavens rejoice, and let the earth be glad;*

*Let the sea roar, and the fullness therof.*

*Let the field be joyful, and all that is therein:*

*Then shall all the trees of the wood rejoice*

*Before the Lord: for He comes,*

*For He comes to judge the earth:*

*He shall judge the world with righteousness,*

*And the people with his truth.*

Then, crouching down, with David leaning over me to guide the sapling to its destination, I planted the little silver birch tree. Next to David stood Paula, Virginia and Linda and Richard Horn. Cardinal Lustiger would have been very proud.

And Latif Freedman would have been very proud, too, for our ceremony was also in honour of his new life. Maryam, his daughter, told me that the silver birch was his favourite tree; he used to love going to see the trio of silver birches near the winter garden in the Botanic Gardens. No wonder ... the silver birch is so mysterious, lovely like the moon, revered by the native Canadian tribes and used to make their canoes.

**7 April 2000**

Getting ever so much closer to Benigna. We did a lot of gardening and planting today. I think she really would like The Little Sisters of Joy to succeed! We put a lot of dahlias round 'the' tree.

**19 May 2000**

**Return from Israel**

Everything went well with my trip to see Maryvonne. She has settled in Jerusalem and has got involved in her course in the Ratisbonne Institute. I was able to see her only for a very short time, but something important was resolved. She confessed to me that she hadn't really told me the truth when she wrote to me last Yom Kippur and said she could no longer 'walk on my way'. The real problem was that she couldn't live the Vow of Poverty and I can understand how difficult this would be for her.

In some ways I have been preparing for this all my life, when I loved Linda more that my own blood family, left home and shed possessions and baggage along the way. Even the selling of my house in 1986 and the move to live with Benigna was a preparation for what was to come and my life now, although I couldn't see the whole story at the time.

Maryvonne and I talked for a long time in her little house in Jerusalem. When we were finished, we went out into the street and she put her arm round me, like an uncle would do to his favourite niece, and gave me her blessing. When she left me, I sat for a very long time on a bench in the open air and felt utterly peaceful.

**27 May 2000**

**Closure**

Under the guidance of the Holy Spirit, David and I have entered into our annulment process. It means we can both be free. I could have gone on as we were, but it was important for him that he was able to get married again.

When I went to Norwich to give my first testimony under oath, I had an amazing grace-filled experience. The priest showed me into a room at the Cathedral. When I entered, there was a tape recorder on a low coffee table and beyond it there was an oval table with a cross at the window, which was looking out onto a lovely garden. On entering this room, I had a massive sense of déja vu, which always means to me that I have arrived at a point of time in my life when I am exactly where I am meant to be. Anyhow, I found it very reassuring.

The priest asked me a lot of questions and I tried to answer as truthfully as I could. He plied me with cups of tea but, at the end, spotting a decanter with some alcohol, I dared to ask if I could have a drop and, knowing what I had just gone through, he was happy to agree!

**14 July 2000**

Since I decided to write my autobiography as a closure to David, I have been hard at it. I am feeling mentally shattered as I am doing so much writing at the moment. Must keep going for another week and then I can start the typing.

**20 July 2000**

**Concert**

I've got a very important new friend to invite to the party. Natania came into my life today when Benigna was hosting the little concert for Magen David Adom, the Israeli ambulance service which also helps the Palestinians. She has been doing it for years and it is a really good cause. It also brings members of the Cambridge Jewish community together through music. I am singing, with Benigna at the piano, and Margaret Allan is playing the cello.

I was on the door, waiting for the people to arrive, when a bright, good-looking young woman of about 30 appeared. Someone told me that this was Natania, a singer in her own right and someone I would instantly get on with, especially because of the music. We hit it off right away, and have arranged, amongst other things to go to a concert of Russian music in Corpus Christi Chapel.

**10 August 2000, 11 pm**

This has been a really beautiful evening. The Russian concert was divine. I think I was particularly inspired because I have Russian blood and I feel the emotions of the songs so deeply, even if I can't understand the words. And it was such a lovely mixture of the sacred and the secular.

The unexpected always happens. Natania and I were chatting at the end when a young woman with a beautiful Slavic face came up to us at the end. It turns out she is a friend of Natania, is Polish and her name is Ania. She seems to be at a loose end at the moment so I have invited her to Newton Road. If the weather continues like this we can sit in the garden.

**20 August 2000**

It has been a wonderful evening. After quite a long chat in the dining room over tea and cake, Benigna discreetly withdrew and left Ania and me to talk in the garden. We seem to have quite a lot in common and we are both at a crossroads in our lives, which always seems to make for a strong friendship. She is from Cracow and her mother and brother still live there. I've got Polish Jewish blood, so I guess we are both 'Middle European'. Ania is a quiet person, which is good for me, so it looks quite promising.

**10 September 2000**

Dorothy has come to stay from Liverpool for a week. Last night she listened while Benigna played and I sang. I went right through my repertoire, from *He Shall Feed His Flock* by Handel, to *Down by the Salley Gardens* by Britten, to the Italian arias and Fauré.

I don't think that I have ever sung better; I sang with a passion and joy, responding to the love and amazing gift of listening which Dorothy possesses.

**27 November 2000**

Sometimes the nuns in Grange Road celebrate Mass in their little oratory inside the convent, rather than in the beautiful but austere chapel in the grounds. It was a happy day for me today that I joined them, for I happened to be next to a Sister I didn't know and whom I really 'met' when we were down on our knees in prayer!

The nuns are in 'transition' and Sister Jennifer (as I later discovered her to be) has been brought up to oversee what is going to be a big move after over 60 years in Cambridge. Sister Jennifer is tall and willowy with a lovely smile and is an expert on the Septuagint, the original Greek translation of the Bible. She seems like someone I would be able to confide in.

## 15 January 2001

David has taken away his pianos from the 'Box' at the bottom of the garden and has said I can turn it into a chapel. Benigna has given her permission too. I have bought a four feet marble slab from a local stonemason and we are commissioning a woodcarver in Bottisham to provide the base of an altar, so that we can have Mass there. All very exciting! Especially as Mr Frost has suggested we carve some Hebrew letters in the base.

In the meantime, I am decorating the walls with some pictures, in icon form, of the Virgin Mary, which were given to me by my beloved Svetlana before she died. Benigna is giving me some lovely red curtains and the Sisters in Grange Road are donating altar cloths and candle holders. I have to remember it can't be done overnight. It will be interesting to see who comes and prays here. Sister Jane in Brookside, always a close friend, has donated a stunning ebony and ivory crucifix.

## 15 February 2001

### Clare Priory

Out of this first meeting, Father Billy Baldwin, my mentor, looking at my Rule, covered practically every aspect of religious life: *Authority, Prayer, Obedience and Government.* He has told me that no Bishop will accept a Rule without Constitutions, so I must get started on those! I will need some help.

I feel I am in good hands. And so wonderful to be taken

seriously. He just poured out his wisdom, gained from being an Augustinian for all these years and from working in the prisons and with divorced and separated Catholics. Augustinians are so practical! That's what I am finding from my new friend Sister Jennifer, too. Father Billy says the key to our way of living is the humanity of Jesus.

## 29 February 2001

This morning it started snowing as I was out walking the dog. Clare came to stay last night, in the tiny end room where I do my writing (it was Ash Wednesday) and this morning we greeted each other very warmly.

I laughed as the snowflakes fell, feeling very happy, and in my heart I was singing a line from one of my favourite modern hymns, *Let me be the Christ child to you*. Two children came up to pat the dog and it felt like Narnia.

## 1 April 2001

I have just met a charming Augustinian nun who is half Spanish. When I told her about Father Billy and the Constitutions, she offered to give me a copy of some of the writings of her Congregation, so that I may get some idea of a layout for my own. I have set about the task in the little spare bedroom to the right as you come up the stairs in Newton road, which is directly opposite my own at the far end of the corridor. I am sitting at the little table and facing west.

## 14 May 2001

### Eve of the trip to Poland

A little while ago I went to the big Church to make a confession.

I was going away and was afraid that something would happen in the next few days that I couldn't handle. There was a strange voice on the other side of the curtain. The priest said he could not absolve me ahead of time of something I hadn't already committed. *'Can't you at least give me a psalm to say?'* I asked him. *'What about Psalm 23?'* he replied. *'I can say that one in Hebrew,'* I said. *'Are you a Jew?'* he asked. When I said that I was, the priest said that I must come and visit him in Cracow to see where the Jews were carted off to Auschwitz.

Now it is evening and Jeremy, the retired Anglican Bishop of Papua New Guinea and nephew of Benigna, has just had supper with us. We all had a good laugh because Vlad (my Polish priest friend) phoned to check the last minute arrangements for going to Poland in the morning. He asked me how I would recognise him but wasn't too pleased when I said he could wear a flower in his buttonhole. He said there would be lots of clerical looking gentlemen at the airport but I would be sure to recognise him.

**15 May 2001**

**Cracow**

And recognise him I did: he was smiling and a bit portly, just as I remembered him. He asked me on the way to the seminary, where he is in charge, to quickly tell him my life story, as his colleagues were asking, *'Who is this Gila?'* So I did my best and, by the time we got to our destination, he was well primed.

What a welcome! A beautiful suite of rooms, on the ground floor of the seminary, flowers and fruits everywhere! The seminary is in Bernardinska, in the heart of the city, in a beautiful leafy street with the castle on one side and the magnificent Vistula river at the end. I feel quite at home already.

## 17 May 2001

I have been taking my meals with the priests in their private dining room. Quite a privilege! Vlad has asked me to move places tomorrow and I said I was happy to do so. When I asked why, he said the Bishop was coming and I had been sitting in his place!

## 18 May 2001

## The Bishop

I was very nervous in the morning and put on a new skirt. Eventually the Bishop came at noon. Although the seminary is in Cracow, he is the Bishop of Sosnoviec. He was tall and imposing with a rather dramatic, carved face. Vlad introduced me by saying, *'This is Gila and she is a Jew!'* The Bishop replied by saying, *'I like Jews!'* and I knew he meant well. The conversation between us turned to Hebrew and Israel: the Bishop had studied in the École Biblique in Jerusalem, and then he seemed to run out of things to say. He looked down at his plate, then looked directly at me and said, *'Do you like vodka?'*, and the men fell about laughing because they knew that I had spent the previous evening drinking vodka in a nearby bar.

At the end of the meal, the Bishop did me the great honour of reciting the Grace after Meals in English.

## 19 May 2001

I have completely fallen in love with this city and almost with one of the seminarians, too! His name is Gregory and he has been appointed by Vlad to show me round. Gregory, who is a mature student and whose English is perfect, explained to me in the castle that the furniture was floated down from Gdansk in the north to Cracow in the south. There are many legends in this city and it is hard to keep up with them. Vlad took me to a Mass in honour of John Paul II in the castle (Ania met him when he was Bishop of Cracow), and I commented on the fact that everyone wore their cassocks here. As we were struggling up the hill to the castle Vlad said quite firmly, *'Don't make fun of my cassock, I am going to be buried in it!'*

## 20 May 2001

It is definitely providential that Ania is visiting her mother in Cracow at the same time as I am here. Today we arranged to meet and have a coffee in Kazimierz, still known as the Jewish quarter, although there haven't been many Jews living here for some time. After the Holocaust, the Polish government forced the Jews who were still living there, or who had returned, to leave in 1968.

Legend has it that King Casimir, who was kind to the Jews around 1600 and let them into Poland when they were being chased out of Europe and being blamed for the Plague, had a Jewish mistress called Esther. In true kingly style (and with biblical overtones), he asked Esther what he could give her. *A quarter where my Jewish people can live in peace*, she replied. And so Kazimierz was born. It is very vibrant, certainly with a Jewish atmosphere in its coffee shops and restaurants and places where they make Klezmer music, and with a strong sense of history. Ania and I had a szarlotka, a Polish apple cake, and then we took a walk through the city. We passed the tram cars and were trying to get to the other side of the street. Suddenly, Ania grabbed my hand like a child and rushed me to the other side. We came to a church and I said to her, *'You know I have had the feeling that the city is going like this to me,'* and I hugged my arms around my body. *'Well,'* said Ania, *'it could be a clamp, or … an embrace.'*

And I knew it was an embrace and I had a strong sense of *coming home.*

## 23 May 2001

Vlad is away today-he is teaching in Częstochowa. He took me there briefly yesterday and said a private Mass for me in one of the side chapels. He talked about God being hidden and our quest being about bringing Him into the light. He bought me a beautiful icon of Jesus to replace the one I gave away years ago in Cambridge.

Vlad doesn't want me to become a nun; he thinks it would change my personality. While he was away, his colleague was in charge and said how nice it would be if I came to live in Cracow and could teach the boys Hebrew! I felt very happy and honoured.

## 24 May 2001

### Auschwitz

Vlad had told me that he visits Auschwitz to remind himself that he is capable of these atrocities as well. So it was with some trepidation that I accompanied him in the car to the camp. It was quite surprising when I got there though.

The thing that I noticed first was when I went to the toilet; various instructions were written on the walls in Hebrew and Polish. For some reason I found this disturbing. I made my way to the barracks where many Jews had lived, but also Polish priests; there were photographs with names on the walls. Some Jewish music was playing on the intercom and a rather sad man, who seemed Jewish, was sitting near me. As I listened, it was as if I could feel Israel rising from the ashes and this sense of

Resurrection was to stay with me throughout my visit to the camp.

I hurled myself at what was called 'the Wall of Death' and shouted that nothing could overcome me. I had a sense that I was going to sing in Auschwitz and it was when I was in the part near Maximilian Kolbe's cell, amid the steel and concrete, that I lifted my voice and sang *Eli, Eli*, about the transcendent God who never ends. This piece was written by Hannah Senesh, a young Hungarian Jewess who emigrated to Palestine in the 1930s. When war broke out, she volunteered to fly a plane behind enemy lines in Hungary. She was captured and put to death by the Nazis.

Sometime when she was living on a kibbutz in Galilee, she wrote the words of *Eli, Eli* as she was walking by the Sea of Galilee. She also wrote:

*The souls of those who have gone before us light up the way for the rest of mankind.*

Vladimir looked on as I knelt down at Kolbe's cell, adorned with a few flowers, and paid my respects. Kolbe, who had exchanged his life for that of a stranger who had a family, particularly annoyed the Nazis because he led the prisoners in song and apparently kept on singing as he was dying. Again the power of Resurrection was very strong.

We went on to the camp further up the hill, but all that I could sense from it was a sort of dreadful limbo. Apparently John Paul had said Mass there, but it didn't feel very like a consecrated space and I was keen to return to Cracow.

On the way back, we picked up a couple of students and, to lighten the mood, we went to the place where the Pope had been born and ate a special cake, which the local bakery made in his honour. Then we went to the house where John Paul had lived. There were some of his diaries under a glass case. I couldn't help noticing that his handwriting seemed identical to mine.

## 26 May 2001

The highlight of the trip was the invitation by Vlad and his sister to his niece's first communion. Magda is a beautiful child of about ten years old and it was a special event for me. It was in the local village church and I sat beside Vlad's father, a small and kindly man, dapper in his blue suit. The children were all dressed in white (it was amusing to see the little boys in their white plastic shoes!) and Vlad gave the sermon. He demonstrated the miracle of the Eucharist with a loaf of bread and several interesting gestures; of course, I could only understand a little of what he said, but the children were enthralled.

Afterwards, we went to his sister's house. Vlad told me that it was in this garden that he had told his father he was going to be a priest. His father had been digging the garden at the time and didn't even look up when Vlad gave him the news but kept on digging. Now we all sat round a sumptuous table, full of Polish delicacies. I was made to feel very welcome.

 Vlad's father was beside me. We discovered we could speak German together. Suddenly he turned to me and said: 'I had a lot of school friends.  One day they all disappeared. *Poles, Jews, we are all just children of God, aren't we, Gila?'*

When I walked outside later with Vladimir, I suddenly noticed that everywhere there were fruit trees.

**19 June 2001**

**Beata meets Benigna**

I laid out a nice tea in the garden. Just when I had given up on her, Beata arrived late. You could see in her eyes beauty, healing, gentleness, acceptance and contemplation ... I had to say something! When I said she had very beautiful eyes, she recounted how, at the age of 15, she was away abroad with her parents. A Russian man came up to her and said how beautiful her eyes were and wanted to take her away, but she was restrained by her parents.

Afterwards, we talked about her timidity (underneath I think she's really quite strong) and how she's taken on big tasks: running for election and becoming a doctor. I seized my chance. *'Have you ever thought about becoming a nun?'* I asked. *'That's the kind of thing you think about in holidays,'* she replied.

Benigna came out and they chatted happily. When Benigna went in, Beata asked me whether I would recommend her to go to Auschwitz. I had told her of my recent experience. Apparently her Polish father had been helped to escape by a Jew during the war. I said that I wouldn't 'recommend' it, only if God wanted it. Beata went into the house for a moment so I had time to think and when she emerged from inside, I said, *'Children go to Auschwitz; I think you should go.'*

She sat on her bike at the gate and said how much she'd enjoyed talking to me. I put my hand on her shoulder and said goodbye.

**27 June 2001**

I phoned the marriage Tribunal and Mrs M. said that the first and most important Tribunal had AFFIRMED our application for annulment. Isn't that so beautiful? The Church is affirming that our lives can continue in this way. I can freely pursue my vocation, and David his life with Rebecca and little Paul.

Nonetheless I shed tears of emotion. Loss, grief, relief and probably a million other things. After the phone call, Mary, the lodger and a fellow Catholic, saw me coming out of the room. I told her what had happened and she said that David would always be my friend but that I was being guided.

## 28 September 2001

I couldn't decide yesterday, on Yom Kippur, whether to go to Mass or to the Synagogue. I decided to go to Mass. When I arrived at the large Church, there was Father Robert and he was at the lectern, saying, '*Today is Yom Kippur.*' And all my friends gathered round me and hugged me and said, '*We are so glad you are here.*'

## 4 October 2001

## Maryvale

I have just attended the inaugural lecture here in Birmingham of a distance learning programme in Catholic Theology. I heard about it months ago, applied, took fright and changed my mind. Then I went swimming one night, happened to chat about it to a lady in the pool who said in a very forceful voice, '*You have to go!*' and swam off. So I applied again and here I am.

The man who gave the lecture is called Dr Francis Clark. As he was speaking, I felt as if a dart of love was coming into my heart and I felt that was the reason I was here. He is gracious, gentle with a wide view of Theology; apparently he was a Jesuit, was wounded in the war, married and has written a book about his life called *Godfaring*. After the lecture, I spoke to him, said I was a Jewish convert and told him a little about *The Little Sisters of Joy* which, of course, is still in formation. He has asked me to write to him.

They all seem very nice people. The Director of Studies is a gangly man called Father John and apparently an Anglican convert. Fierce on the outside but I am sure soft within! There is a charming couple from Barrow-in-Furness, Nick and Martina; when I said aloud I was in need of a holiday they immediately invited me to their place, which is on the edge of the Lake District, in a rather more hidden part.

The curriculum is challenging: one 5,000 word essay a month and three or four residentials here in Maryvale. This is where Cardinal John Newman lived shortly after becoming a Catholic when he was forming his community, here in the '*Vale of Mary*'. There is a beautiful chapel, with a statue of Our Lady which has the words in Latin above it, '*Mary is completely beautiful.*'

## 7 November 2001

All this Peace and Reconciliation must be on my mind because last night I had an interesting dream. I dreamt I was walking up Brooklands Avenue with David and Benigna. When you get to the top the road forks to the left and the right. The road on the left appeared like a pool of blood. David and Benigna slipped away to the right and I kept walking through the pool. I was unafraid and in the morning I just noted it.

## 14 November 2001

I struggled, in an exhausted state, down to see my mother in the Jewish care home in London. Sam, my brother, appeared for five minutes and I hugged him. It was a good feeling. I asked him to find some photos of my paternal grandparents. All I know about them is that my grandfather was a cabinet maker from Minsk, in Belarus.

But it was a meeting on the bus from the home to Golders Green that was the highlight of the day, and a rather humbling experience. A Jewish woman got on the bus – aquiline nose and dark complexion. She obviously knew I was Jewish too. She was from Dublin, but had been in London for 60 years with odd trips back. I revealed I was from Cambridge and she asked what I did there. *'I'm studying,'* I said. *'What?'* she asked. *'Theology,'* I replied. *'What's that?'* she asked. *'To do with God,'* I answered. *'I can't see the point of that,'* she countered. *'I just open the prayer book and believe what I read.'* And then she quoted something I remembered from my childhood and that I used to sing – I remembered the melody at Golders Green station.

*The heavens belong to the lord*

*And the earth he gave to man*

*It is not for the dead to praise the Lord*

*Nor those who go down to the silence*

*But we, we bless the lord*

*From now and forever*

Then she said, *'God reveals certain things to us, but the rest He keeps to himself.'*

As she rose and got off the bus, she said, *'Be well, sei gesund, sei gesund.'*

**26 November 2001**

Today our annulment was finalised. Sister Jenny and I were together in the afternoon at the Grad Pad (the University social centre) and we celebrated. This quiet nun in her sixties is the source of much strength to me. The letter from the Church said, *'You are now free with the Church's Blessing to enter into a second union.'*

Later I read the letter to the friend who had brought me and David together in 1982 and told her that the conversation, begun in mid June 1988, in which I announced to David that God was calling me out of my marriage, was, 13 years later, now at an end. *In my end is my beginning.* I decided to throw a party for my close friends.

**8 December 2001**

**Goddaughter**

It's the Feast of the Immaculate Conception. As at the Assumption, Mary confers many graces on this feast. Eleanor has just been baptised and confirmed into the Catholic Church, so I have my first goddaughter. I met her in the University Library and she told me that she was doing a PhD in history, played the clarinet and was thinking of becoming a Catholic. And she was from Baltimore.

The highlight for me was when I held up the candle to her and gave her the Light of Christ. She kept saying afterwards what a beautiful candle it was, and, indeed, it came from Walsingham. Benigna did a heroic job on the organ and I sang the Et Exultavit with feeling. Father Robert, Terry, B and I all sat round to a rather messy but congenial supper with Eleanor looking supremely serene. Praise God!

Notre Dame Cathedral, Paris, where Gila met Cardinal
Lustiger in 1999

Planting of silver birch tree in garden of Newton Rd,
January 2000

Clare Ranson in Bethlehem

Gila on her 50th birthday at
Newton Road, December 2001

Gila and Benigna Lehmann in
the 'Upper Room' at Newton
Road

Ania Norman at home

Cracow 2001 - First communion of Vlad's (Fr. Scoczny) niece. Gila and Vlad's father front left

Tim Bennett, Friend and
Neighbour

Mrs P. (Lydia Paschalis) owner
of the Regent Hotel

Silver birch tree in the garden
of the Haven

Eleanor Stewart, Gila's Goddaughter

Gila's mother, Dorothea, January 2004

Bishop Pearse Lacey, Bishop
Emeritus in the Archdiocese
of Toronto with Gila

The author with The Moving
Swan - Memoir Part 1 2006

Israeli celebrating Shabbat in
the Craft Market

**12 December 2001**

**Fifty years**

Something really beautiful happened last night. I celebrated my 50th birthday, in the presence of close friends, in Benigna's drawing room at Newton Road. Before all the guests came, Beninga and I lit the candles together – it was also the second day of Chanukah, so a great grace. I was wearing my long blue kaftan.

It was an unusual party, as I had asked the guests to do a party piece and most of them obliged. My new goddaughter played the clarinet with Benigna at the piano, and Fardijah, her daughter, played *The Hippopotamus* (very apt as I identify with hippos) on the double bass, and the sound filled the room. Sat was there, along with Linda and Richard, and Ania and I played a duet on the piano; I think they found it quite touching.

Father Edward Booth, my Dominican friend, excelled himself with a skit he had written himself on the Religious Life and Sister Jenny rounded off the evening with a splendid recitation of Psalm 150 in Greek. Jillian Skerry came and a Polish friend called Agnieska, who chatted to Ania.

Pam appeared – I think she had come all the way from Oxford. I was fretting a bit because she was late. But when she arrived she had a magnificent multi-coloured dress on *'especially for you'*, she said, giving me a bear hug. She also presented me with an exquisite velvet shawl in red and orange.

Perhaps the pièce de résistance was the contribution from Clare, my beloved *'Daughter of the Heart.'* To my great surprise and delight, she had prepared a long eulogy, in the style of *The Lord of the Rings*, about our various times together. She wove a wonderful tale of our friendship in her beautiful poetic way, ending with a quote from a Lebanese poet:

*Let your best be for your friend.*

*If he must know the ebb of your tide, let him know the flood also.*

*For what is your friend that you seek him with hours to kill?*

*Seek him always with hours to live.*

(Kahlil Gibran)

Just before my birthday, I went to visit my elderly friend in the Hope Nursing Home. She had just gone blind and said it was the best thing that had ever happened to her, as she was making a whole new bunch of friends that she had not been able to make before. It was her 90th birthday. I asked her how I should live the rest of my life. She paused for a moment then said, *'Just as you have always done.'*

## 2 January 2002

Benigna has been ill over the past few days; it is as if she had been at the bottom of a deep ocean and she only 'surfaced' at 2 p.m. yesterday, when, strangely enough, Rachel (an old friend whom I associate with healing) rang for the first time in two years. I had a reaction to B's illness when I woke up this morning and realised that we might have come close to losing her.

As I was writing about Pam and that she might come to join us in a letter to Maryvonne, Pam rang and said, *'Sister Gila!'* I was really glad to hear her and said that B was well enough to receive her. I had the feeling that she, too, was relieved. Waiting this morning was as difficult as ever, although there was plenty to do – dog walking, etc. I read a nice children's book. The birds are hopping about on the snow-covered lawn and the sun is bright. Pam arrived at 2 p.m. and who knows what will happen from then on? We are held tight in God's hands.

I have just read something else which came from an Indian Festival last year:

*In JOY we are born*

*In JOY we live*

*And*

*In Death it is to*

*JOY*

*That we return.*

## 1 February 2002

Pam has come to live with me in community as a Friend. She asked me if she could do all the shopping and the cooking, if I did all the religious bits, like looking after the chapel. Of course, I said yes, secretly thrilled, and this evening she made a beautiful meal in the upper room for Benigna and me. Pam is a mysterious bird, a phoenix rising from the ashes.

She is also a larger than life character; adopted into an American Catholic family, she discovered she was born into a family from French Canada, and is now in the business of tracing all her relatives on the Internet. She has discovered that her great grandfather on one side was a trapeze artist who fathered nineteen children in abject poverty, while her great grandfather Bernier, on the other side, was a famous Arctic explorer, whose annals are written up, complete with photos, in the prestigious Scott Polar Institute here in Cambridge. Her own work, mapping the Jewish communities of the Middle Ages, including those of Cambridge and Oxford, is unique, to say nothing of the humorous and fascinating talks she gives when she takes people round the medieval Jewish quarter here, which extends between the Round Church and the Guildhall.

I happened to be in the Guildhall the other day and discovered that one time it was a Synagogue. I don't think any of the Mayors have been to one and I propose to liaise with the Jewish community and take the Mayor to the Synagogue one Shabbat.

## 7 February 2002

Last night Ania came to dinner and gave me a Polish lesson. Pam cooked a lovely meal. We were all in harmony with each other and this morning I dreamt of the swans in Great Shelford.

## 19 March 2002

### St Joseph's Day, late

Father John from Vietnam has just blessed us in the Garden Chapel. A great event. Benigna was there, of course, and Pam and Clare. Father John had just put on his robes (and rather fine they were too) when there was a scratching at the door and it was Buster, our dog, wanting to join in. So he got blessed as well.

### The next morning

I have just discovered that a girl was born to David and Rebecca in the middle of last night. They are thinking of calling her Anna, which happens to be the name of my grandmother.

**Third Sunday of Lent 2002**

Mr and Mrs Pheasant fly in to have breakfast on the lawn every morning at about 7 a.m. She is much shyer than he is and, when I open the window to throw out the bread, she scuttles away and hides under the clothes line. He is pretty fearless and is strutting around.

Robert gave a great sermon today at Grange Road on the Samaritan woman at the well. It was full of nuances. I am so glad I met him after Father Brendan took ill. He said Mass in the garden chapel for us last night and it was a moving occasion; Benigna was there and also Robert Frost, who built the altar.

Pam's family seem to feel she is living in a wholesome environment (she has described it as *'living in poverty with the Little Sisters of Joy'*) so we must be doing something right. The garden is full of daffodils about to bloom.

**16 April 2002**

On Friday, we gave a *Concert for Peace and Reconciliation* in Newton Road. It had been quite a strain preparing it and galvanising everyone into action. Ania came with her boyfriend Mike.

During the concert, as I was performing, Ania was looking at me with so much love that, on the one hand, I could hardly bear it but, on the other hand, it gave me the courage to go on. Mike talked to Benigna in the interval, which made her happy. We raised £71. The odd £1 had come first, from the little old man who cleans Lucy Cavendish College. On the promise that sometime we would perform *Cavalliera Rusticana!*

I have started reading Laurence Van der Post's *Journey into the*

*Interior.* Last night, I told Pam a lot about Svetlana, my dearest friend who died. A former star undergraduate and actress at Newnham, she tore up her programmes and became a hermit. She was baptised into the Russian Orthodox Church by Metropolitan Anthony and eked out a living by proofreading. She was unable to travel anywhere but always asked me to take her *'in my heart'*. She gave me a long quote from Van der Post about fulfilling one's destiny, in which it said something like you have a duty to try to fulfil your destiny if you have the grace to get a glimpse of it, because that is the only thing that gives life meaning. She died suddenly of a heart attack and is now surely with the angels.

Benigna came and sat in the chapel yesterday at about 6 p.m., a magical time. With her expert eye she moved around some of the pictures and, of course, it all looked better. I think she is feeling happy and involved.

## 1 July 2002

Father Billy has had a wonderful idea. He says I should start an Association of Friends of *The Little Sisters of Joy*. I can't imagine how, but I seem to have gathered about 500 names from over 20 countries, meeting these people on trains, buses, planes, in the street and just about everywhere! I have just composed a newsletter which I am going to send to them, describing all the beautiful events of the past 18 months, when the whole thing started to take shape.

## 18 September 2002

## Poland again

Once again I have been welcomed in the Seminary in Cracow by Vladimir, his colleagues and the boys. The difference this time is that I will be visiting Warsaw briefly, to stay with some friends of Eva's, one of my Polish teachers in Cambridge. Vlad took me out for a meal as he usually does on the first evening, and filled me in with the latest news.

## 20 September 2002

I have arrived in Warsaw after a pleasant journey – Polish trains seem to be very good. I was amused to see that the young men help the old ladies to put their cases on the luggage rack, bury themselves in their newspapers for the rest of the journey and help the old ladies down with their cases at the other end!

The friends of Eva's are very nice with well-behaved children. They live in an expensive apartment and have given me a nice room. After walking me round the local neighbourhood and buying me ice cream, the husband has asked me if I would like to go to the Warsaw Ghetto on Sunday; it took me back a little but I said yes.

## 22 September 2002

It's hard to remember that Warsaw literally rose from the ashes, as it is quite impressive and has been completely rebuilt. We went to the national museum but I found it rather ghastly – too many military exhibits. There are quite a few monuments to the Holocaust in the town. Nothing remains of the ghetto, just a large space with flats built all around. But there are some impressive large stones round what was the perimeter, with inscriptions in Polish and Hebrew. And the first thing I saw was a lady feeding hundreds of pigeons and them flying up to the sky in what seemed like a gesture of Resurrection.

My host and I went round all the stones, carefully reading all the inscriptions. As we approached the last stone, we saw two men bending over it. They turned out to be from Israel, one native born and the other originally from Romania. They saw my wooden cross and asked who I was. I told them I was a Jewish Christian living in Cambridge, England and working for Peace and Reconciliation. *'Does Cambridge need it?'* asked the man from Romania. *'Everywhere needs it,'* I replied. Then he said that he didn't have a problem with Christianity as he was, as a child, employed to ring the bell for his local church on Sunday. After a few more moments of conversation on the theme of peace, he said to me in Latin, *'Dominus vobiscum.'* *God be with you.* I felt deeply moved.

**24 September 2002**

**Back in Cracow**

I am back in Cracow and have just visited the Remu Synagogue. This must be where many of the Jews worshipped before they were taken away, to the ghetto and elsewhere. Vlad had showed me the bus stop which marks the point of deportation. In the Synagogue, I was able to guide three different groups of tourists round, explain what the ark and reading desk were, tell them about the everlasting light above the ark and, conveniently, someone had left a prayer shawl lying around...

When I left the Synagogue, I went to the big square and danced to the sound of an accordion. Again I felt very light and free.

**8 October 2002**

Last night, Father John Minh, the Vietnamese priest who gave us a blessing last year, said Mass for us in the garden chapel. We were about fourteen of us and afterwards Sister Jenny said it was a wonderful place to *'come in from the cold'*. It was a rather wintry night but the liturgy was very heartwarming. The nuns all came from Brookside and afterwards, when we gathered in Benigna's dining room, were only too glad to sample a little of my Polish vodka!

Quite a few people have been down to the chapel and it's nice to think it is a place where they can find some peace. It is down by the woodland and very near where the stream used to flow.

## 1 November 2002

Jenny suggested that I go and see Father Theodore Davey, a canon lawyer at Heythrop, the Jesuit College in Kensington which is part of the University of London. Yesterday, this kind man gave me over an hour of his time, and all free. He said it was the Church's duty to help me. He looked over the Rule and said, *'We don't touch the Rule … that is the inspiration.'* He then looked over the Constitutions, much still to be written, and insisted that, if I was going to have Vows to be renewable every ten years, there must be three years of Temporary Profession, to which I naturally agreed. I had suggested in the Rule that *'By renewing our vows every 10 years we reflect back in faith our past and look forward in faith to our future, making it a living and vital commitment.'*

I hadn't realised that Fr. Davey was so distinguished; he is a man who really lives in the spirit as well as the letter of the law.

## December 2002

We have just nursed Benigna while her broken leg mends. I slept in her little room so that the social services could nurse her in the telly room, where she received many visitors. I have been doing my Maryvale essays on the dining room table, where I could keep an eye on her in the next room. I think her family in America must have been worried about her because they are sending one of her granddaughters over for a few months. I have a strange fear that there are storm clouds on the horizon.

## The Watershed Years, 2003–2004

### 5 February 2003

I am preparing myself to have an operation for breast cancer, something which I have known about for two years but for various reasons didn't want to face until now. A close friend said you always wake up on the second alarm call! I am having a mastectomy on my left breast and some lymph glands taken away in the left arm. While I was being examined, a nurse came in and said that it was going to be a spiritual experience. I never saw her again; it was obviously a message from on high and I will have to work it out in due course. But incredibly comforting.

I have seen the surgeon. I looked at him straight between the eyes and said, '*I know that God is in your hands.*'

### 10 February 2003

I have had the operation and am recovering in the hospital. When I was lying on the trolley, feeling a bit nervous and waiting to go to theatre, the young nurse who got me ready came rushing up and said that she was a Catholic and her Feast Day was that of St Thomas More, the first Saint I ever encountered when I was 14 in Glasgow, and the perfect one to protect me during this kind of thing. When I went into the operating theatre, I asked the anaesthetist to pause for a moment and asked him when I could drink my Polish vodka. '*Well, not tonight,*' he replied.

When I came out from the operation, everyone was laughing and there were several orderlies at my side, all dressed in blue gowns. One told me his name and said he would accompany me to the ward. I have ended up in a gynaecology ward as there isn't the room anywhere else. Everyone seems kind, although the physio is not too good, but you can even get a cup of tea in the middle of the night.

This morning something extraordinary happened. I was sitting resting when a young woman came in. I recognised her from Lucy Cavendish – a medical student from Glasgow and very religious. She chatted to me for a while then pointed her finger and said, like a prophet, '*God knows where you will be this time next year!*'

I had been uncertain about the future, as things have been difficult since Benigna's granddaughter came from the States, but I was quite taken aback. I am going to a private clinic, thanks to Benigna's niece, for a week, to get some decent physio and a good rest, so perhaps things will develop after that. I have also booked a week's holiday in Malta as, before my operation, a friend sent me a card which said, '*Malta is the nurse of the Mediterranean.*'

### 8 March 2003, First Week of Lent

### Malta

I have arrived here at the start of the Gulf War and there is a big TV screen in the lobby of this little family hotel; I am going to try and ignore it as much as possible. The view from the hotel over the Mediterranean is stunning. There is an outdoor pool but it's still a little cold to chance it, so when I am a bit rested I will go into the town and ask the hotels there if I can use their pool. I did some swimming in the clinic in Sussex and they said it is good for my morale.

A lovely couple at the table beside me have said that I should join them as I didn't seem too well. I must say that I am grateful, as this is the first time I have booked into a family hotel and I didn't want to be alone. I don't know what they do, but I suspect it is something religious.

## 10 March 2003

I was walking down the street today when I met two ladies. They asked me if I was Maltese – I was rather flattered! I told them I wasn't and it must be my curly hair and Jewish looks that made them think so. And when I expressed to the young woman in the little hotel bar how much I liked the country, she said, *'Come and live with us, Gila!'*

## 11 March 2003

I was all alone in the swimming pool in the downtown hotel today. I felt strong and beautiful and confident that I was being healed. I have just been to an ancient shrine which the locals claim dates back to St Paul; there are some amazing frescoes on the walls which could indeed have been his. The Maltese are a bit like the Orthodox Jews: they babble their prayers, so I feel quite at home. And I have been to the local Church, very beautiful and perched on top of the hill, overlooking the sea. I am going to ask the priest if I can renew my vows, as I have been doing each year since I met Cardinal Lustiger in 1999, and it is more or less the right time during Lent. I like to do it as we approach the Feast of the Annunciation on the 25th, as this is when I was received into the Church.

## 14 March 2003

The priest was a bit reluctant as, of course, he did not know me, but when I explained my background, he said he would be happy to hear my vows of Poverty, Chastity and Obedience at the end of the morning eight o'clock Mass. The Church looked beautiful with a lace cloth, hand woven and embroidered in purple on the altar. At the end of the Mass, the Maltese priest heard my vows that I renewed for a year and prayed that I would keep them!

It was a beautiful morning, radiant with promise as I emerged from the Church into the early sunlight and I was filled with grace and hope. It was then that I realised in what way my suffering had indeed been a spiritual experience.

'I am the vine, you are the branches,' says Jesus in the Gospel of John (Chapter 15). He goes on to say that the fruitful branches must be pruned to bear more fruit. The whole breast cancer experience has touched on the core of my femininity and made me think about my mortality. With this new strength I will be able to live life even more to the full and give myself more wholeheartedly to doing God's work. And hopefully bear more fruit!

## 19 March 2003

Now that Peter Smith has become Archbishop of Cardiff, Bishop Michael Evans has been appointed the new Bishop of East Anglia. One day I will have to submit my writings to him. It will be a leap of faith.

## 14 April 2003, Holy Week

I recovered enough from the operation to co-host the Seder meal at the big Church as usual. Benigna came with Hannah who, after all the difficulties between us, said a beautiful thing: that she could see that I was steeped in my Jewish tradition and that I should make the New Testament the same. A lovely thought and a lifetime's quest.

There were about 70 people, as usual, and I felt inspired as I sang the beautiful music which weaves through the Seder. With Father Tony at the helm, it was a wonderful way to introduce people of other traditions to the narrative of the Jewish people and, by their participation, to enable them to see in a mystical way the links between the Passover and the Paschal Mystery of Easter.

## 6 May 2003

Something has gone wrong. I have undergone an emotional upheaval, and, for the first time, Pam has found it difficult to understand. Dr Hymas, my psychiatrist, suggested I might like to have a break for a short while and come in to Ward S3 in Addenbrooke's Hospital. It has been a good idea and given me the space to think about things and all I have been through in the past few months.

It looks as if I might have to find somewhere new to live. Dr Hymas has been very kind and helpful. I have been to the council office in the hospital and they say my case is top priority and they will find me somewhere to live as soon as possible. It is proving an interesting year, with many challenges, but I have been given sufficient graces to withstand them.

## 16 June 2003

God works in mysterious ways, his wonders to perform. I am allowed out of the hospital, now that I am recovering and I have been going to the Catholic Church on Walpole Road now and again for Mass. This Church is near the hospital but also very close to where I lived in my own little new house when I first came to Cambridge in 1982.

I saw Father Eugene when he said Mass in the hospital only a few days after my operation and he was deeply compassionate. I have made a new friend also and her name is Margaret. I discovered that they were having a 40-hour prayer session and this was the last day. So this morning I went and prayed for an hour. Then I had a walk round Cherry Hinton Hall, where I used to live. I had the feeling I should go back and make another short prayer.

Something made me say 'Bring my brother Ronnie into the Catholic Church.' It seemed like a fervent prayer, as even my other brother had been worried about Ronnie's spiritual state … he seemed to be in limbo. The last time I spoke to Ronnie on the telephone, he said to me, 'Why are you asking me if I am seeking after Truth at twenty minutes to two in the afternoon?'

I came back to the hospital and they said they had some bad news for me. They told me that Ronnie had just died – he had had a heart attack while he was riding a horse. I knew, in that all-encompassing way that is only of God, that now, after death, all was well.

I recalled how much Ronnie loved horses. When he owned stables and the horses were in the field and he wanted to gather them in, he used to sing Adon Olam, the final hymn of the Sabbath morning liturgy, and they would come at once.

**8 September 2003**

**The Haven**

Today I moved into my new flat. There is a lovely garden, albeit covered in weeds, and the walls are painted red. I have enlisted the help of a Christian family, whom I met when I was staying in temporary accommodation, to help me paint. I have chosen a soothing white and green colour. I am sure the children will do a good job.

There is a large living room which overlooks the garden, off it a tiny kitchen area and a good sized bedroom, with a hallway and tiny bathroom. It is wonderful to have my own place again with a new set of keys. I have decided to christen it *'The Haven'* and to offer it up to the Lord as a place for prayer and hospitality.

Facing the garden is a little wood of trees – I think they were planted about thirty years ago when the estate was new. Birdsong is very loud at 4 am! A pair of magpies has settled in the neighbourhood; difficult birds but a sign of JOY. I have gathered that the area is very mixed, with people from all over the world, but at the moment it is very quiet, with hardly a soul moving about. The flat is also very difficult to find; there at least three ways of getting to it, but it means I will be fairly undisturbed. With a library, post office and two supermarkets, I would hope there is a real sense of community. Parts of this estate don't have a good reputation, but if you have lived in Glasgow you can live anywhere and often what people tell you about the place is not the reality. As long as there is some sort of human solidarity ... Glasgow was magic for that.

Today is a special day for two reasons. Firstly it is the day the Church commemorates the birth of the Virgin Mary to her parents Joachim and Anna (whom I am particularly fond of, having discovered the Virgin Mary in the shrine of St Anne of Beaupré in Quebec in 1988), and also it is the beginning of the Orthodox liturgical year. So I am very blessed. Perhaps the best thing about my move is that I am close to St Laurence's Catholic Church and I hope to invite the priest here once I am settled and share a little of my story.

## 12 September 2003

It is evening and something unpredictable happened in the early afternoon. I was sitting by the big picture window in the living room. I like the view and decided not to put up any curtains. Around 2 p.m. I heard a roaring noise at the window. Terrified, I ran out the front door in my slippers, hoping to follow the chimes of the ice cream van. A young couple was standing on the pavement. Glancing down at my slippers, they asked me where I was going and then suggested I go back home. I felt that God the Father had paid me a call and had decided to make His presence felt, so why be terrified? If He wanted to make His home with me, surely that was a good thing?

When I phoned and told Natania that I was terrified at two o'clock in the afternoon after this experience, she said that anyone would be terrified at any time of the afternoon!

I feel happy about being on the north side of the river. The river by Chesterton Road was the first thing I saw when I came to Cambridge in August 1982. I was staying for a couple of nights in the Ashley Hotel by the Old Spring pub and they told me that if I wanted a meal I would have to go to their sister hotel nearby, the Arundel House Hotel. It faces the river. I remember going into the bar, ordering a drink and feeling incredibly lonely. Then a woman in her sixties came over to me from the other side of the room and said, '*You look lonely, come and join us!*' She was Australian and that gesture of kindness launched me into Cambridge.

I can get to the river in ten minutes by bus (and the no. 1 is quite frequent) or 30 minutes by foot.

**28 September 2003**

Last night I celebrated the Jewish New Year in the Haven for the first time. A friend and I sat round the gate-legged table, drank the Palwin kosher wine and ate apples and honey, as is the custom to make it a sweet new year. I am in touch with Benigna and Pam and they are coming here to see me soon but it really is a new beginning.

**28 December 2003**

I have received many Christmas cards with warm wishes for my new little home. And I have made a new friend. I am settling well at St Laurence's, but the other week I decided to have a change and go to the Latin Mass at the big Church at 6.15. Afterwards, I met a quite extraordinary old lady called Dr Sessions. Very difficult to tell her age or her nationality but she seems Middle European, like me! She seems to have taken to me and has invited me to her home on the river. She told me that her mother was a concert pianist and that when she was growing up, many famous musicians came to her home and even stayed there for a while.

Yesterday, we went to the beautiful garden in Grange Road and sat in the winter sunshine. When I told her about *The Little Sisters of Joy* and that I was a musician, she turned to me and said, '*You'll have to start singing for your supper!*' I had been *singing for peace* with Benigna, but suddenly it came to me that I could return to my singing with the guitar – there is a large repertoire of music from the 60s, and it would be continuity with my youth.

I started thinking about Dr Landau, the gynaecologist who brought me into the world after my mother had such a difficult pregnancy. And her son, Oliver Sachs, a well-known American

Jewish psychologist. He was an atheist but apparently he said that Music, Love and Prayer make for an integrated or fully-rounded human life. Was this my chance to combine all three?

## 22 February 2004

Last night my dream came true when I gave the first *Concert for Peace and Reconciliation*. The venue, by kind permission of the Master and Fellows, was the beautiful chapel of Clare College. As I was rehearsing *Donna Donna*, a song about freedom, written for the Yiddish musical theatre and translated into many languages, a Jewish lady who turned up early said she had not heard it for forty years! I took it as a good sign. My old friend Mrs Gee appeared just as I was about to begin and I waited until she was in place before commencing the concert. Amazingly, there were about forty people; I had done most of the publicity by word of mouth and it had obviously paid off.

I sang, with feeling, a mixture of songs from the 60s, folk songs and Jewish music, some of it from the Synagogue, and the combination seemed to go down well. For some reason, when I sang *Donna Donna*, I stopped singing at one point, but the audience continued on its own and I became aware that something special was happening. I am giving myself time to reflect.

When we gathered in the beautiful ante-chapel in the interval, an elderly man said his favourite song was *Erev shel shoshanim*, a love song which apparently is used by belly dancers all over the Middle East!

I concluded the concert with *Psalm 133* and got the audience to sing in parts. The psalm says: *hinay ma tov umah naim shevet achim gam yachad*. Behold how good and pleasant, a tribe of brothers living together in unity!

Dr Sessions couldn't be there, but I held her in my heart and privately dedicated the concert to her.

**1 March 2004**

It seemed an appropriate moment to plant a second silver birch tree. This time I wanted it to be a hidden event. I enlisted the help of my social worker, a very nice guy they assigned to me after my mini breakdown last summer. He went to all the trouble of driving me out to the same nursery in Fordham that Benigna and I went to get the first birch, so a sense of continuity. He is also big and strong, so he dug a hole and put the sapling into the ground in the left hand corner of my garden, while I recited some appropriate words. He is not religious but he respected what I was doing and I think he appreciated the meaning of it.

**4– 11 April 2004, Holy Week**

I am absolutely exhausted, as I have co-hosted two Seder meals this week. The first was with Father Dick in the Catholic parish hall, with about 70 guests. Throughout the evening I felt quite inspired when I was singing and filled with the JOY of the Chassidim. When we opened the door for Elijah, to herald the Messiah, a man, whom I can only describe as one of the '*Blessed are the poor in spirit*' came in … we thought the Messiah had come!

When I did it for the Baptists in Great Shelford on Thursday (there were eighty people at that one), I opened the proceedings by saying, '*Tonight your minister has two wives.*' (Rev. Beardsley's wife was sitting on the other side of him at the top table.) They all laughed and I think it got the whole thing, which they were unfamiliar with, off to a good start.

I was very touched, as the tables were laid beautifully and with great care and for the *charoset*, representing the bricks and mortar the Israelites had to use in Egypt, they had found a recipe, new to me as well, which comes from the Sephardi tradition. And they really rose to the occasion, because Baptists can sing! I sang the Hallel Psalms with them at the end and there was much JOY. There is a tradition that Jesus sang these psalms with His disciples at the Last Supper but, of course, Jesus was not mentioned and they had to see the connections in a mystical way.

I knew that Rob had been taking his congregation through Lent and that this was to them a sort of culmination, so I felt very honoured.

**Easter Monday 2004**

Hectic and all that it was, I have had a little time to reflect in this holy season. It suddenly came to me that the Rabbis have a mystical concept called *Tikkun ha-Olam*. It means '*repairing the world*'. Could it be that when the audience was singing in the concert in Clare it was a form of prayer, rising up to God and effecting a form of healing on the world? The music too was about justice, righteousness and freedom. And after all it is attributed to Saint Augustine that he said, '*He who sings, prays twice.*'

**8 May 2004**

I am making my third trip to Poland. I was a bit apprehensive beforehand, but once I was on the plane I felt I had come home. It was only four days after Poland had joined the EU and they said they were looking forward to coming into the West. Don't come too far, I thought, or you will lose the beauty of the East.

I received such a beautiful welcome from Father Vladimir and the young seminarians that I wept. Everything is green and the sun is interspersed with thunderstorms, the kinds that go boom, boom and seem unique to Cracow. My bad Polish seems to be understood and I am being hurtled round a series of religious events. I talked to some students in the large square and prayed in a tiny church where some ladies were saying their May devotions.

**9 May 2004**

Vlad and I had breakfast alone together and I was able to fill him in about my journey and Cardinal Lustiger, Bishop Peter and the story in general. He listened carefully and then said he was going to take me see his Papa and my beloved friend.

Once we got to his father's little flat, Vlad relaxed, took off his shoes and we sang a little. It reminded me of the time on one of my previous visits when he had driven me into the mountains and all the way he sang songs, off by heart, from *Fiddler on the Roof*. If I remember correctly, it was approaching Friday evening and the Sabbath was falling fast. I kept thinking, as I was driving, how like my brother Ronnie he was, with that jovial personality and our fraternal relationship.

Papa opened the door to his balcony to get some fresh air and, as we stepped out, there was a magpie on the grass. Papa and I had a wonderful conversation in German and it was as if the years had rolled away.

Map No. 1 Gila's Journeys

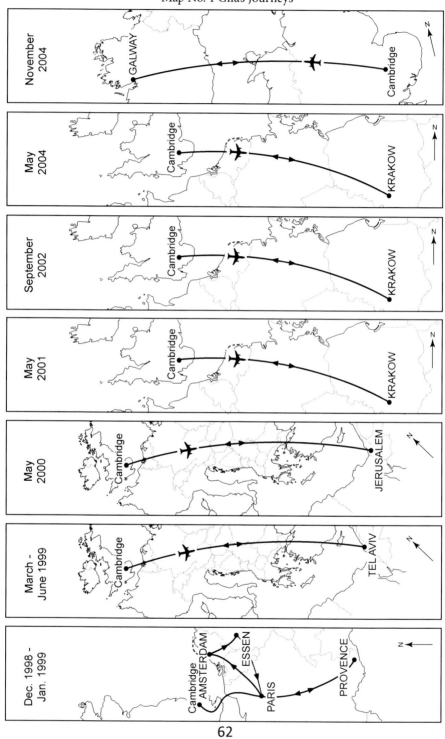

**10 May 2004**

The Jagiellonian University in Cracow is stunning, with beautiful ancient courtyards and an atmosphere of deep learning. I discovered there was a Copernicus Museum in the Old Court. There was a little hassle about getting a ticket, but I succeeded and was accompanied by three Russians, one Pole and two Germans. This stretched the linguistic skills of Daisy, our Bulgarian guide, to the limit, but somehow she bravely managed.

We saw many treasures (some of which had been taken away during the war, said Daisy) and a glass case with a beautiful monstrance for Adoration of the Blessed Sacrament. Daisy explained that there was a long tradition of celibate academics who were very religious and combined study with prayer. They would also have long conversations about the meaning of life.

When we got to the rooms where Goethe and Schiller had passed through, I got down, to the amusement of my fellow tourists, on my knees, in a gesture of thanksgiving: they had been my heroes when I was studying German at Glasgow University in my wild youth in the 60s.

In the last room, the *aule*, the Grand Hall, I prayed by the window where they used to lecture in theology. You can touch the stone with one finger, said Daisy. Then the Polish man said to me, '*Don't you think that Cracow is the most beautiful city in the world?*' I said, '*Yes, with Jerusalem, they are linked together in my heart.*' And the Polish man was happy and another man wished me *shalom aleychem* and Daisy sang a beautiful song from Serbia.

**11 May 2004**

This morning after breakfast I had an upset stomach. I think it must be all the emotions of the past few days. Everything is very intense when I come to Poland. I managed to get some medicine from the local chemist (the lady spoke good English) and then I trundled to the Post Office. It was good to be in an ordinary place with ordinary people. They were all a bit downcast, like in any post office, but there was a lively assistant who appreciated my sense of humour and a nice man who had '*heard Pani speaking Polish*' and who lent me a groschen.

Outside in the hallway we all waited while there was a downpour and several claps of thunder. I chatted to a charming elderly couple from Cracow-he was a retired orchestral conductor. The lady asked me if there was thunder in Cambridge and wished me good health. The love with which the couple looked at each other was very moving.

Went back to the seminary and back to bed. The thunder started again. I suddenly felt very protected and cosy, just like a child, with the bangs and a little lightning going on all around. I thought: this is what Ania must have felt as a child. I slept well.

**12 May 2004**

The boys had been complaining to me that their schedule was very heavy and there was very little recreation during their long day. I said I would speak to Vladimir about it, although I thought that probably there was very little I could do. I was surprised when Vlad invited me to give a concert yesterday evening to some of the boys. There was a guitar I could use. He thought it would be nice if it could be in the upper room. One of the Priests had found a Torah scroll in a disused loft outside Cracow years before and had brought it to the seminary, where it was proudly displayed in a glass case in this room. The view from the window in the evening was beautiful with the gentle waving of the trees.

I sang many Hebrew and English songs to Vlad, one of his colleagues and fifteen or so seminarians, including my selection of love songs. They liked *Donna Donna* particularly. The boys gave a hearty rendering of *Psalm 23* in Polish. Vlad took the guitar and sang a Russian ballad. All evening he looked relaxed and full of JOY and it was obvious that they all enjoyed it.

Something made me play *Vetaher Libenu*, a lively song about consecration to God's service: Vladimir waved his arms around in a Chassidic dance and what with the Torah scroll, the black cassocks and the *Simcha*, the JOY, we could have been back in the time of the Baal Shem Tov (Leader of the Chassidim, a Polish movement in the 17th Century, who prayed outside in nature and were centred on JOY).

**17 June 2004**

**University Library, Cambridge**

I am sitting three floors up in the South Wing, where two days ago I discovered in the book stacks all the Theology books I would need for the rest of my life … and beyond. I was so excited that I got down on my knees in gratitude and thanked God. I suddenly felt the need to express this to someone and, as it happened, a middle-aged man with a nice face was passing by. When I told him, he exclaimed, '*Hallelujah, praise the Lord, my dear! I'm a Baptist Minister!*' He turned out to be an Australian by the unusual first name of Horton and his church is in Teversham. He is interested in the Project and wants to receive the newsletters.

**Later ...**

It's nearly 6 p.m. now and I am still here. I was praying the Evening Prayer when the strong sound of singing wafted through the open window; all I could make out was that it sounded like an Oratorio, with a lot of rejoicing and hallelujahs! How could I know all those years ago that God was preparing a way for me beyond my wildest dreams?

**10 July 2004**

Just completed another Residential at Maryvale. Tucked away behind the main chapel, up some very narrow steps, is the oldest Sacred Heart Chapel in England. Not too many people know it's there. Occasionally I meet Andrea, a Religious Sister from Glasgow, and a close friend, in this tiny chapel because it's the quietest place we can meet. One night I couldn't sleep and went into the main chapel. There was Andrea, almost in the dark and huddled in deep prayer. I was in the balcony and didn't want to disturb her, so I tiptoed out and went to bed.

**29 August 2004**

My friend Kitty rang me and asked if I would go and visit Elena Sumbatoff. This lady, now bedridden, has a very interesting history. She is Russian, although she was born in Italy. She developed polio at the age of nine, didn't receive the right treatment and lay on her back for many years. A Russian Priest organised for her to go to Stoke Mandeville Hospital, and there they got her upright enough to sit in a wheelchair. With her love of classical ballet she was able to direct ballet dancers from her chair, making movements with her hands to show them what to do. She also loved folk singing. She taught ballet to local children in Ligorno and, when she moved to Cambridge, she had a visit from the great Nureyev.

I went this morning. She greeted me warmly from her bed, on which were four stately cats, all of different colours. They seemed to be guarding her. We had a lovely chat and I shared with her my Russian origins; she was deeply interested. I asked her whether she would like me to come back next week with my guitar and she was very enthusiastic.

## 8 September 2004

## The Haven

Father Robert said Mass here this evening, on the Feast of Our Lady's birthday. There were about seven of us, including Sister Jenny. It was a blistering hot night so we opened the back door. Robert was rather solemn. Just at the moment we were all partaking of Communion, the cat, Mickey, as if on cue, came in from outside and ate his food too! Jenny and I could hardly contain our laughter and all in all it was a beautiful celebration.

## 9 September 2004

Just visited Elena again with my guitar and she absolutely loved the Jewish music. A curious thing happened as I was leaving. I had explained to her that I wouldn't be back next week as it was the Jewish New Year. As I was going out the door, she called to me, '*When did you say the _head_ of the year was, Gila?*' I had not used the Hebrew words, Rosh Hashanah, which means _head_ *of the year*, so she either knew the term or it came straight from her subconscious.

## 21 September 2004

I never did get back to see Elena. She died this morning and is now surely with the Angels.

## 18 November 2004

Sister Benedict invited me over to Kylemore again at just the right moment (I submitted my writings to the Bishop a little while ago) and I have just returned from a glorious week there. I flew to Dublin then Galway and it was an hour by bus from Galway town to the depths of Connemara. It was after eight in the evening when I finally arrived with my large rucksack. Sister Benedict met me at the bus stop and we drove to the Abbey. She apologised, but my room was at the top and did I mind the climb?

I consoled myself on the way up that it would all be worth it, the long journey, etc., and there was bound to be something nice when I got there, and, sure enough, the room was full of flowers and fruits and they already made me feel really welcome. I slept the sleep of the just and woke up in the morning to find the light flooding in and that I was surrounded by mountains!

In the dining room I met a very nice priest from Letterfrack, a village nearby. Sister Benedict came and checked on me from time to time, to make sure that everything was alright, but the highlights of the trip were the times I was able to spend with her, in between her busy life of prayer and running the small farm.

I enjoyed each evening, going round and feeding the hens in a pair of old spare boots and chatting to her while she did various things in the kitchen of the old farmhouse. I was with her one day and having some tea when I found myself banging my hands on the old and worn table and shouting, '*This is it, Benedict, this is the real monastic life ... I can just feel it!*'

Sister Benedict was most proud of a Victorian garden which had been allowed to fall into disuse and which they were gradually returning to its former glory: quite a big task. I enjoyed watching Benedict talking to all the volunteers and the special smile she had for the young men!

Mother Magdalena, the Superior, allowed me to talk to some of the nuns in their private parlour and they seemed very interested in *The Little Sisters of Joy*. I had asked her if she would do me the honour of reading a copy of the Rule and Constitutions I had brought with me, and when she had finished, she said to me, *'This is an important document – it has a Beginning, a Middle and an End.'*

## 26 November 2004, 8 pm

I was in the University Library early this morning, intending to stay for the afternoon as well, but something made me want to go home early. I remember telling the man at the entrance desk. When I got home, about three o'clock, there were two letters on the mat. One was from the nice village priest I had met in Kylemore and the other was from the Bishop. I decided to open the letter from the priest first. It was an interesting letter, telling me how pleased he had been to meet me and enclosing his sermon for the following Sunday and asking me if I liked it. It was quite extraordinary. It made the same point over and over again. Jesus was rejected, Jesus was despised, Jesus was insulted, Jesus was abandoned, etc., etc. I read it closely and turned to the other letter.

It was from the Bishop, and it was a rejection – a bit of a strange one. There were some very kind things in it: the Bishop told me to carry on with the Peace and Reconciliation, but at the same time he felt I hadn't 'suffered enough' to set up a Religious Community, although he said that he knew that many nuns and priests were supportive of my efforts. He made it clear that there would be no welcome for such a project in his diocese.

Naturally I was devastated and phoned Benigna's house in the hope of speaking to David, who sometimes still visited there and played to Benigna on her piano. And then the miracle happened – David answered the phone! *'This is not even a hiccup,'* he said, *'this is an opportunity. To explore the ecumenical dimension of community.'*

Suddenly I feel as if I am in a whole new ball game.

## 27 November 2004

Clare and I had fixed our own retreat day in Clare Priory for today and it was very appropriate that we chose the theme *'Do whatever He tells you'* from the marriage of Cana. It is the first miracle of Jesus, when he changes water into wine, and it also illustrates the special relationship of Mother and Son.

I had brought my guitar and we sang and prayed, and I was able to get a little perspective on the events of the previous day.

## 1 December 2004

### *Last night I had the strangest dream* (Ed McCurdy)

### The Vision

In the early hours of last night, I awoke, longing, for some reason, to hold a piece of music in my hand. I went a bit sleepily into the living room and my hand fell upon a book called The *Canadian Book of Catholic Worship*. I vaguely remember buying it in a charity shop. I took it back to bed and then spent the next few hours reading and weeping. It contained all my favourite songs and hymns from all over the world. Some were new and composed, for example, by *The Little Sisters of Jesus*; there was one from Edith Stein's birthplace of Breslau and many, many more. All the seminal moments in my life were being presented to me.

In wordless pictures, images and symbols, I felt my life was converging to a single point: **Toronto**. After this wrestling with the Divine through the night, I assented to this Call in the depths of my being.

I slept fitfully for a few hours. When I awoke in the morning it was around eight o'clock. I went into the living room and it was the first frost.

## 11 December 2004

### My 53rd Birthday

Things are beginning to pan out quite nicely. This seems to be a special time of grace, similar to when I wrote the Rule of Life. The presence of Our Lady seems to be very strong this Advent and a young woman who runs the Michaelhouse Centre in Trinity Street feels that Mary is birthing something in me. It seems I must use the Association of Friends of *The Little Sisters of Joy* as a basis for something a bit more expansive: a Foundation for Peace and Reconciliation which is truly ecumenical as it encompasses the *'known inhabited world'*.

I have composed a Foundational Statement, which I will show to certain close friends for their approval. It goes as follows:

### Our Mission

a) To build bridges of peace among all men and women, as our common humanity is the most precious gift we have.

b) To build bridges of peace between Jews and Christians, for it

is from the same Stock that we both come.
*Hear O Israel, the Lord our God, the Lord is One.* (Deuteronomy 6:4)

c) To build bridges of peace between Christians of every denomination, shape or hue, being all in one body, that is Christ.

d) To build bridges of peace between all faiths, for we all have one Master.

I have adopted a new verse from the Bible, to encompass our aims:

*The harvest of righteousness is sown in peace by those who make peace.* (Letter of St James 3:18)

**14 December 2004**

Last night I had a very beautiful experience. I was asked by the Michaelhouse Centre to open an exhibition of linocuts with my singing. The exhibition is entitled *Images of Hope.* Many years ago a Jewish schoolteacher, who had Israeli and Arab children together in her school, asked them to illustrate their impressions of the Arab--Israeli conflict. These extraordinary linocuts are the result.

I sang Peace songs in Hebrew and English and I think they were quite pleased. This place was a church for 800 years and it has been recently refurbished in part as a café. Last night, the people sat round the tables while they listened and it took me back to my late teens.

The old chancel is still there, as is the mediaeval chapel which adjoins it, which is full of light and from where you can hear the sounds of King's Parade. It would be a privilege to sing in the chancel one day.

## 19 December 2004

I have just received a letter from a priest friend in Cambridge to whom I had written in the wake of the letter from the Bishop. He says he feels sorry for my distress and says at the end of his letter that he still thinks that *'your basic inspiration is sound'*.

## 26 December 2004

After my experience in the middle of the night, I was beginning to wonder if God wanted me to take a group of different Christian women and move to Toronto, to set up a community there. John, my philosopher friend, and his wife, had invited me to supper today. They suddenly started talking about Toronto, where he had worked, and the fact that their daughter had been born there. I jumped up off my chair and started walking round the table several times (a habit of mine at important moments) and then the whole experience of Toronto poured out of me.

John offered to contact a priest in Toronto he knew and see if I could touch base with him if I made a trip over the Pond. And perhaps get some help. They dropped me off in Crowland Way, by the little path at the swing park. It was already dark. For the second time I saw the moon, ringed with its corona, as I had seen it around this time in Pomeyrol in 1998. Again I took it as a sign, a form of affirmation that I am on the right path. It is the Feast of St Stephen.

## 30 December 2004

Andrew White, the Unitarian Minister, came to the Haven this morning and approved the Foundational Statement. He says it has a *catholic keel*. I like that image because it reminds me of a moving ship, going safely towards our common destiny, like the Universal Church from which all this inspiration comes. And I have put everything under the Patronage of Our Lady, due to this special period of grace.

Later in the day, I crossed the river and went to the home of Dr Irene Elia, my very dear friend and supporter. We go back a long way, to the days when I took services in the Reform Synagogue (around 1986) and I have had many shared meals there, particularly on the Jewish festivals.

Irene is an anthropologist and a psychotherapist and her husband is Professor of Nutrition and Metabolism at Southampton University. I read out the Foundational Statement to them in their upper living room and they gave their approval. I feel very humble and very proud at the same time. What a wonderful way to end the year and herald in the new one!

## 10 February 2005

The weather is very wintry with snow in places. I suppose I shouldn't have been disappointed when not too many people turned up for my concert in Pembroke College chapel last night. A friend was very good and showed the people to their places and handed out programmes. I think I sang fairly well, but the real concert actually took place the day before.
I was rehearsing in the staggeringly beautiful Wren Chapel when the cleaning lady came in and was worried that she would disturb me. I insisted that she sat down and listen to the music. I sang at my best (she was a good listener) and she really enjoyed it.

**25 February 2005**

Hélène has just come to tea at the Haven. We met at Fisher House, the Catholic Student Chaplaincy. I spotted her in the upstairs dining room after Mass. For some reason she seemed like a kindred spirit. She is studying something called Neo-Latin, which sounds a bit peculiar, but she is enjoying it. She is French, from a suburb in Paris. She is religious and has a special talent: serving on the altar and assisting the priest. It will be lovely if my plan for having a Mass in Hadstock, where the altar from my old house is now stored, takes off.

I like Hélène very much; she is quiet and gentle and I like her parents, too – I met them last week when they came here for a visit. We drove to Grantchester for tea and cake at the Orchard Tea Rooms. Her mother speaks good English, unlike her father, and they are easy to be with. We took some nice photos by the river.

Hélène knows what I am doing. I think it is unlikely she will become a nun but, for the moment, she is walking alongside me. There have been other companions before her – Pam, Paula, Clare, to name but a few – and there will probably be others after her, unless it becomes clear that this is not what God wants.

**1 March 2005**

Father Billy died on 20 February. His heart finally gave out – he was always overstretching himself by going back home to Ireland and going to lots of ceilidhs! I was unable to go to his funeral but it took place, with an apparently good crowd, at Clare Priory, where he lived and was much loved.

I met again Sister Eileen, who has a close relationship with the Priory and lives nearby. When I told her I had moved over the river in Cambridge, she said, 'Have you opened another House?'

## 27 March 2005

Last night at 9 pm, Hélène and I went to the Easter Vigil at the big Catholic church. It was a very joyful occasion and humorous too: when the curtain, covering the large statues, finally came down during the course of the Mass, it was pure MGM.

Afterwards, she came with me to my bus stop in Hills Road and we waited and talked for a very long time. Eventually, she said that she didn't think a bus was going to come – she had room at her place, so would I like to come and stay the night? I said I was a bit worried about leaving the cat but I agreed and we walked the short distance to St Barnabas Road, where she was in some rather nice student accommodation. She slept on the couch while she insisted I took her bed; it was very late and I slept rather fitfully. About 7 in the morning I called out to her, 'Are you alive?'

We had a very simple breakfast and the love of God flowed between us, and we could have been His disciples sitting on the shore while Jesus cooked us fish in the days of Resurrection. 'I knew I was going to spend Easter with someone,' Hélène said. 'But I didn't know it was going to be you.'

I got back to my flat about ten and opened the door. The cat was there and looking straight at me as if he was smiling and his coat was glowing in what I can only call his Resurrection colours of burnished reds and golds.

**31 May 2005**

**Feast of the Visitation of Mary to Elizabeth**

The Bishop of Brentwood gave his permission for us to hold a Mass in the 17th century barn of Hadstock Hall in Hadstock, home to my dear Jewish friend Laura and the present home of the altar, which I had moved there when I left Newton Road. Hadstock is just outside the boundary of the Diocese of East Anglia. It's an interesting place, where St Botolph, the present Patron Saint of travellers, also left his mark. Behind the place in the barn where the altar has been resting, is the wall of the ancient Parish church.

Father Anthony, who received me into the Church in 1989, kindly agreed to say a Mass for Peace on this lovely Feast. Laura and Benigna were the two guests of honour. I sang, Clare read and Hélène served alongside Anthony on the altar. Hélène felt reassured that everything was being done properly and she served in her usual quiet way. Clare read splendidly and Anthony gave a magnificent homily on the theme of Peace. Laura prepared a lovely tea on the lawn and we all chatted happily afterwards.

**10 June 2005**

I am very excited because Margaret Parry, whom I met in 2003 in St Philip Howard Church, has agreed to give the Foundation's first talk on Peace and Reconciliation. And what better person to do this! Margaret is a retired teacher, from Impington Village College amongst other places, and perfectly suited to lecture on '*Peace and Reconciliation from the Biblical Point of View*'. I have chosen a rather fine place to have this talk and today something poignant happened as a result.

I had arranged to see the Bursar of Darwin College, to see if I could hire the Old Library. He was running a bit late and asked me if I would mind sitting in the Reading Room while I waited. For some reason, in the last ten days since the Mass, I have been feeling under pressure as the Project grows, and I could really feel the peace of this beautiful room, which overlooks the garden and the river.

Two men, one middle-aged and one older, came in and started to read their papers. They propped them up so that I couldn't see their faces. Suddenly I began to weep uncontrollably. The older man put his paper down and was very concerned, asking me what was the matter. I blurted out that I was working for Peace and Reconciliation, which was very stressful, and that if only I could come and sit there from time to time it would be a great comfort.

The man said that he was one of the founding members of the College and that I could come and sit there whenever I liked. He got up to go. I was so struck by his generosity that I got to my feet as well and asked his name. *'My name is Dr Joffe,'* he said. *'Are you Jewish?'* I asked. *'Yes, I was born in Jerusalem,'* he replied, and the conversation came to a delightful end.

## 1 July 2005

It is a great grace to hear forty middle-aged ladies, from different Christian traditions, singing *Blowing in the Wind* to the strains of my guitar! We were gathered in the lovely Westminster Chapel, at the end of the Backs, and I was able to share some of my thoughts on Peace with them. I read Isaiah 2:2–4 about universal peace and the mountain of the Lord, which has such a deep meaning for *The Little Sisters of Joy*. The passage about beating the swords into ploughshares reminds me of Elijah and Mount Carmel.

# Map No. 2 Gila's Journeys

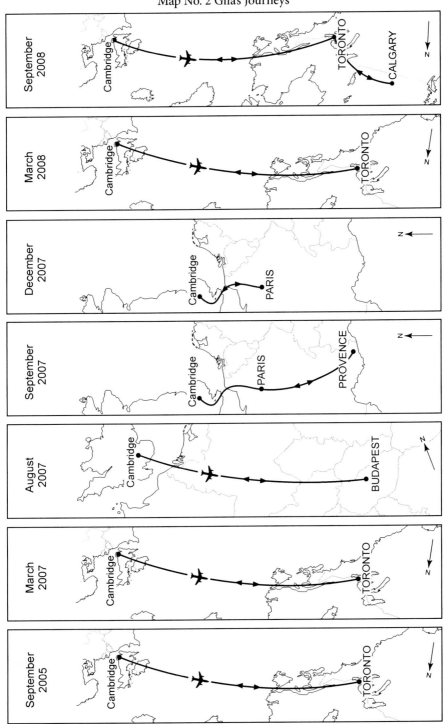

Elijah seems to be very prominent in the hidden part of my life at the moment. So many momentous things have been going on. I see the mystical experience and the call to Canada as part of a wider call, a call obviously stretching back to before I was born but, more practically, from my Baptism in 1989 and, even more, from my Confirmation on the same evening. The Church teaches that you are given a mission when you are confirmed. I think it lay a bit fallow in the first ten years, but now it seems to be blossoming.

**28 September 2005**

I have just completed my first trip back to Toronto since 1988! What a wonderful experience! I have fallen completely in love with the people, the city, the green spaces and the libraries.

John, my friend from all those years ago, told me that his friend was going to lend me an apartment in Bloor and Keele, at the west end of the city. But for the first few days I would have to stay in Dufferin (where many of the new immigrants settle) in the guest house of a rather smart retirement home. It gave me the chance to look round this ethnic neighbourhood and, on the Sunday at Mass, I discovered many Portuguese people and a delicious bakery. Also the local library, where the librarian was Jewish and very kind.

Once in the little basement apartment a few days later, I felt really happy. It was snug, with a bedroom, living room and open plan kitchen. The neighbourhood was quite leafy and I soon discovered a Catholic church at the bottom of the little hill I had to climb when I got out of the subway. It is called St Joan of Arc and there is a lovely priest from New York. After Mass, I went to the sacristy to meet him and he admired my hat! It was a baseball cap a kindly 'gentleman of the road' had given me outside the big Catholic church back home; Father John now told me that it had been specially made after 9/11 by the New York Police Department as a gesture of Peace.

Father John was sympathetic to my cause and gave me the name of one or two people that might be able to help me.

First, I thought I would follow up the contact that John in England had given me. His name was Father Jonathan Robinson and he had founded the Oratory in Toronto, taking Cardinal Newman as his inspiration for a community and parish. John had emailed him from Cambridge. *'What do you think the chances are of bringing a group of women of different Christian traditions here to Toronto?'* he apparently asked Father Robinson. Father Robinson replied, *'Difficult, but not impossible.'* Now I remembered that I had emailed him about myself too, from the local library in Arbury. After I had sent the mail I went out into the little square; I suddenly felt as if the world had stood still.

At the beginning of my trip I was actually in the room with him, in Toronto. He listened intently to my story and then suggested I go to a place in Northern Ontario, a Community, to get some inspiration. He very kindly gave me the fare.

The journey, in the heart of the Canadian Shield, was fascinating. For four hours on the bus I saw nothing but trees, with a glimpse of a tiny hamlet now and then. My experience once I got there was difficult, as the people seemed to have a completely different way of doing things to my own ideas of Community, but I was grateful to Father Jonathan for taking an interest, whilst realising I would have to find my own way.

Canada in the Fall is incredibly beautiful. My cousin Ann, with whom I had spent many happy visits in Drumheller, near Calgary in the west of Canada, had told me of another cousin, Gordon, who actually lived in Toronto. He proved to be very kind. I told him I wanted to visit the Niagara Falls and he said he would take me.

It is an hour and a half's drive from Toronto with many beautiful places along the way. We stopped at Niagara-on-the-Lake and I saw the two blues of the water, where the blue of the lake meets the blue of the Falls. Further along we took an elevator 200 feet down to a gorge and I wept because of its beauty, the trees, the opening out of the landscape, the colour of the water, the gorge and the transition from England to Canada, which was still taking place. Gordon watched me sympathetically. '*What can you see on the other side?*' he asked. 'I see a bank,' I replied. '*That's America,*' he said.

Close to the Falls we discovered a Buddhist Temple and at the Falls we discovered a plaque, with the same name as that on the Temple, which was inscribed: *Niagara Falls has been designated an International Peace Site.* I met a Spanish girl who had just walked the Road to Compostela. '*This is my Compostela,*' I thought.

Back in Toronto, I enjoyed walking round the University district, with its beautiful campus and many places to eat and meet people. I discovered the Robarts Library, which houses the seventh largest collection of books in the world, with its lovely restaurants and open spaces for the students to sit, as well as its main reading rooms, with views over the city. I discovered Felicity, the librarian of the reference section, who spent hours with me researching things I needed to know. Best of all, the Robarts is open to everyone.

I had nice neighbours in the flat and once, when we were sitting outside in the little garden, I shared with them a little of what I was trying to do. Putting feelers out to bring a religious community here, I told them. They said they were not religious, but they seemed sympathetic.

I had a walk through the town and down a side street I found a beautiful church. Apparently it's the Carmelite Church. It also seems to be home to the Chinese Catholic community in Toronto. I thought I could spot someone in the sacristy; turned out to be a warm-hearted priest called Father Paul who is from a congregation called the Spiritans, formerly known as the Holy Ghost Fathers. They work in the countries with the poorest of the poor. Father Paul was intrigued by my story and we met again over coffee at the Art Gallery, where he told me a little of his own history.

One day I went to meet a friend in a restaurant. Right across the street was Massey Hall, a popular theatre. A crowd had gathered before the show. I couldn't help mingling with them and I got chatting to one or two people. It came out that I was a musician, giving occasional Concerts for Peace and Reconciliation. *'Are you coming here?'* one or two of them asked, obviously genuinely interested. I felt deeply touched, and I thought, *'I might, I just might.'*

Now I am back. You can never be too sure of God's Will, but I am going to start the formal emigration process.

## 22 November 2005

The day of Margaret's talk has dawned. I feel excited and honoured that the Mayor, Councillor John Hipkin, has agreed to come. I shared a platform with him when there was an Interfaith Service in Great St Mary's on July 10th. I felt privileged when they asked me to lead the Peace. We were giving the Freedom of the City of Cambridge to the German town of Heidelberg, with whom we have been twinned for 40 years. I have just discovered that it was also the 60th anniversary of VE and VJ Day, when war came to end in Europe and Japan.

**Evening of the same day**

The talk was a great success. Margaret excelled herself when she drew from her rich knowledge of the Bible to show how it could be a basis for Peace and Reconciliation. The Mayor showed a real interest and asked many questions. We were a small but diverse group from the Christian, Quaker and Muslim traditions. The Old Library was an inspiring venue, we had tea and cakes and, at the end, a gentleman from the Quakers gave a moving and impromptu speech about Peace, which drew the whole thing together. It had been worth all the tears.

**13 January 2006**

The year has turned and, as Archbishop Peter had said in his Christmas card to me from Cardiff, it's going to be an exciting one!

Last November, I paid to get reading rights in all the Federation libraries. This afternoon I returned to the library in Westcott House (where they train Anglican ordinands) for an intense session with the Maryvale coursebook on Eschatology, and was rewarded by finding a pre-Vatican II handbook which explained 'The Last Things' (Death, Judgement, etc.) rather succinctly and beautifully.

As the light began to fade outside the heavily leaded windows, I knew Shabbat was approaching. I went out to return the key to the office to find the door locked. Facing me was a steep staircase, with a light emanating from the door at the top. I climbed the stairs and noticed it said '*Principal*' on the wooden door. I knocked and a warm voice said, '*Come in!*' So I stepped inside to a large cosy room and said '*Shalom*'. I put out my hand and said I was a Jewish Roman Catholic with reading rights in the Federation. The Principal, a gentle, good looking man, said his wife was a Catholic and hadn't he seen me at the large Catholic church?

Back outside together, I said to him, *'Do you know what it is right now? It's Shabbat!'* And he said did I know what Rabbi Heschel says about Shabbat? All week we are trying to be in control of the world. On Shabbat we let go, we are not in control and we rest. As a human race, we will eventually move from striving into resting. So I said that I had done enough striving in the week and I was going home to rest. *'You do that,'* said the Principal – and I left.

## 17 January 2006

I had already noticed on the map that there is a Swan river in the west of Canada, in Saskatchewan. Also, possibly in Alberta, the Swan Hills – both of which I would like to visit one day.

Last Saturday, I popped into the Oxfam bookshop. One of the attendants overheard my request for Canadian books and produced a book on homesteaders at the turn of the 20th century, some from the US, living in incredibly harsh conditions. One lady wrote a diary about her and her husband's carving out the beginnings of a new town from the barren land, with the help of a Scandinavian family. They put up a makeshift kitchen and she provided them with all the meals.

The book fell open at a page with a black and white photo, quite extraordinary, of some Russian women drawing a plough with their bodies, young and old, over a dozen in harness. They were doing it to spare their exhausted animals. The caption on the facing page was mentioning a poetic piece about them.

*They were singing ... no, actually, it was weeping.* (Goes on to describe the incredible sound.) *And the Swan river was glistening beside them.*

The lady in the bookshop knew nothing about the Sisterhood, but said, *'Isn't emigrating a bit like homesteading?'*

I asked a lady on the bus if she knew exactly what homesteading meant and she said she thought it was building a home with some land all round it – the land was important.

**21 February 2006, 9 pm**

Anthony has just celebrated Mass for some of our Associates at the Haven. He celebrates the liturgy so beautifully and we are in the week of Prayer for Christian Unity. He took the first reading from Nehemiah Chapter 8. Judaism has been reconstituted after the rebuilding of the Temple by Nehemiah, and Ezra is reading the Torah to the people, who are weeping. He tells them not to and says, *'In the Joy of the Lord is your stronghold.'* I adopted this verse for *The Little Sisters of Joy* very early on in the project. Even in Israel in 1989, I was given a small sign. I went into Christchurch, the earliest Protestant church in the Holy Land, near the Jaffa Gate. It was empty, apart from a woman sewing by a grand piano and, when I went up to look at the Bible on the lectern, it was open at this verse.

**1 March 2006**

I translated the French Rilke poem which is going on the frontispiece of my memoirs today, partly because I didn't want to reproduce the translation, whose author is unknown, and partly because I just wanted to do it. In the end I simply changed a few words, but it made a difference and I will put, *'Based on an unknown translation which inspired me'* at the bottom.

**19 March 2006**

I am in the Regent Hotel, which is a haven of peace and tranquillity. Now they are just finishing breakfast. I had a good chat with Mrs P., who is the owner of the hotel, which is run with a group of charming receptionists and staff from all over the world. The hotel is really an icon of old-fashioned Italian hospitality and I have taken to spending a lot of time here, mainly on my own, sometimes with a friend and from time to time with a group of Associates to celebrate our anniversary on the Jewish New Year for Trees.

I am drinking tea, before going to Mass at the big Church, and gazing out of the window which overlooks Parker's Piece. To one side is the swimming pool, behind which is Hughes Hall. On the opposite side of the green is the fire station, adjacent to the police station, next to Barr Ellison, where I signed my will last Wednesday.

Further down is Robert's house, Christ's Pieces and the bus station. Straight in front of the window are some very beautiful plane trees, with some branches overhanging the green. Crisscrossing the green are long sandy paths where the people are passing slowly. Bicycles are going to and fro in the distance. White birds dot the green with a blue bus in the far distance.

**21 April 2006**

It swept over me today that Dorothy is dying. She has been such a good friend, even though things were difficult when I went to see her in Liverpool. But she had enough strength then to take that lovely photo of me with guitar for the back of the book.
No more tears. I cried myself out some time ago. But Christ is risen! And I am on the verge of a whole new life.

**9 May 2006**

Only one of the ladies from the Impington Mother's Union knew the pain I was in last night, as I wasn't sure if the books would arrive in time for the launch of my little book, *The Moving Swan*. The church hall looked lovely and they had gone to a great deal of trouble to make things nice. They had agreed to help me launch the book; it all came together after they had heard me singing at a previous meeting and it was much better than if I had done it on my own.

I started the presentation about my life, encouraging the fifty or so of my friends who had gathered to join in the folk songs and Hebrew melodies. Pam was an absolutely star; halfway through she entered, stage right, carrying thirty brand new books. Afterwards I signed and sold about twenty and we all had a delicious tea.

**11 May 2006, 4.30 am**

The dawn is just waking. It is just over two days since the book launch. The blessings (as Latif once said, once you are on the right path) are beginning to flow. Last night my neighbour, Tim, came in. I told him quite a lot about my life, especially the care work, and we got to talking about the book. I asked him what the cover (two dancers, violet skirts, arms raised-by Degas) suggested to him. He didn't make the connection, as some do, with Swan Lake but said it was '*two ladies dancing*'.

**22 May 2006**

Quite a few hidden and beautiful things happened today. A Jewish friend came round and we had a lovely quiet talk; she told me that some years ago she had been an artist in residence in the Arts Theatre. She asked if the JOY of *The little Sisters of Joy* was connected to the Chassidim!

**25 May 2006**

**The winds of change**

The last few days have been a real watershed. I visited my mother Dorothea in the Jewish retirement home in London. She seems to be retreating and going on some sort of inner journey. I had to feed her, but this is something I have enjoyed ever since I looked after the old people on the kibbutz in 1999, and I felt it was a real privilege. I am sure she is dying so I am preparing myself.

Mum comes from such a distinguished family, among them Henri Bergson, the philosopher, and Jonathan Miller, the opera producer, and my maternal grandmother, who was Swedish, was the only grandparent I knew. My relationship with my mother is very close – it's as if she is the rock and I am the lichen so it's going to be hard. But my brother Sam has been very devoted and pops in every day to see her; he lives close by, so she is in good hands.

**20 June 2006**

Yesterday I went to see Peggy, David's mother, in the home. I took her a copy of *The Moving Swan* and she was thrilled. We sat by the window and, despite her Alzheimer's, we had a pleasant chat.

**28 June 2006**

My mother has died at the age of 97. She was buried today beside my father and my brother Ronnie in the Jewish Cemetery in Bushey, just outside London. I chose not to go to the funeral because things have been very difficult between me and my family in the last few weeks and I want to preserve the memory

I have of her when I saw her recently.

She gave me my faith, my music and my openness of spirit towards my fellow human beings. I believe I have also had an experience of her after death, but it is too soon to speak about this. I am hoping and praying that things with my family will soon be healed.

**29 June 2006, After Mass at 8am**

**Feast of St Peter and St Paul**

Strange and wonderful how things happen. I had arranged a Mass for my family quite a while ago and it now seems very timely. I hadn't realised what an important Feast this is; it really honours the two Jewish pillars of the Church and it is heartening that the Jewish dimension is always mentioned.

**20 July 2006**

**Little Gidding**

I felt very honoured to be invited by the couple looking after Little Gidding in the depths of Huntingdonshire to a weekend reflecting on the troubles of Israel/Palestine.

This place has been a community twice; founded by Nicholas Ferrar in the 17th century, it was a place of deep prayer for several families for 25 years, until it was threatened by the Civil War. My favourite poet, George Herbert, Anglican clergyman and mystic, was attached to this landscape which seems to be in the middle of nowhere and is timeless and has been described so beautifully by T.S. Eliot in his *Four Quartets*.

A small but varied group, we exchanged our experiences of Israel/Palestine, some revisiting their happier memories. A lady called Marisa spoke movingly about the programme of *'Accompaniment'* of Israelis and Palestinians of all ages in which she had participated, often under distressing circumstances. Marisa lives in Cambridge and seems a very righteous person; I hope to get to know her better. I also made friends with Joy, a lady in her seventies who lives near Croydon and has asked me to come and stay with her.

The small church in the grounds is radiant with the presence of Christ, even now that the second community, living there also for 25 years up until recently, has also left. Above the sanctuary is written *'Pray for the peace of Jerusalem'*. During the Evening Prayer, on a beautifully sunny Sunday evening, I sang in Hebrew with my guitar. The door was open and facing into the light. Afterwards, four of us danced a *horah* outside on the lawn, as a spontaneous expression of our JOY.

**23 September 2006**

Rosh Hashanah. The New Year. A time of renewal when we turn towards the Creator. I wonder what this year will bring?

**15th October 2006**

God is a God of surprises. I walked into a new café called Victoria a couple of weeks ago, to be greeted by a lovely girl behind the counter. Her name is Alexia; she is French and she is a student of business at Anglia Ruskin University. She comes from near Paris and is here for just a year. Apart from the weekend at Little Gidding, I have been quite miserable since my mother died and this meeting was quite a consolation. I have been going there quite regularly since and Alexia told me tonight that when she first met me I talked a lot in rapid English – she couldn't understand most of it, but she could see I needed to talk!

The café is owned by a Chinese family; actually they seem more like a dynasty as it is dominated by a rather ruthless lady, but the Chinese man in the shop is friendly and he wants to read my little book. Alexia would like a copy, too, and I'm glad that the book is proving useful.

I will meet her boyfriend soon; he is coming over from Paris to see her. I am going to pluck up the courage to ask her if she wants to come to some of the colleges with me.

**31 October 2006**

I was invited by a group called the *Grovebury Ladies*, all local, to sing and play in the Arbury Community Centre. About thirty ladies sang the songs of the 60s with me. In between, I talked about *The Little Sisters of Joy* and our mission and I think they were moved, especially when I read out the passage from Isaiah 2:2-4 and the dawning of universal peace. They were also interested in the book and at the end I signed copies for some of them.

**November 2006**

At last some harmony is restored in our family in the aftermath of my mother's death. Yesterday we had the stone setting, the second ceremony in the Jewish religion which follows up to a year after a funeral. My brother had invited me and greeted me as his sister as I entered the prayer hall. We went on to say some prayers round the grave. Afterwards, I realised that three Rabbis attended the ceremony; the two 'extras' wanted to honour my brother by coming.

During tea in my nephew's house afterwards, I met a charming man who had been an assistant to the Chief Rabbi. He heard my story with great respect.

## 5 December 2006

How very fortunate to give a concert in such a lovely space! Last night went very well in Robinson College Chapel. I had planned it carefully, but there were some wonderful surprises. Those amazing Piper windows in greens and yellows, not at their finest in the dark, but which remind me of Chagall and Israel! And that marvellous acoustic – no wonder I sang well!

Marisa had told me she would be very tired, but she was there, my two daughters of the heart, Clare and Louise, were shining at me from the front row, and Alexia was busy selling programmes and the odd book. I sang her favourite song, which is *Last thing on my Mind* by Tom Paxton. Afterwards, she told me that she couldn't understand all the words but she could tell the variety of emotions I displayed by the way I sang and she said that that was important.

An unusual thing happened apparently in the interval. I had asked if the bar could be open and the college had agreed. Everyone from the audience went in and ordered drinks and then mysteriously smoked salmon sandwiches appeared from nowhere!

I was feeling energised and was actually waiting in the chapel for the audience to come in for the second half. I sang well, encouraging them to sing and somehow it was a lovely dynamic and quite a mystical experience.

Alexia Lagosanto by the Seine
in Paris

Dr. Irene Elia at the Haven

Gila and silver birch on Bloor Street, Toronto

Translator Françoise Barber at the Haven

Sister Benedict, Kylemore
Abbey, Connemara
November 2004

Gila with guitar entertaining

Fr. Piotr Kisiel (1966 - 2013)
Parish Priest of the Polish
community in Cambridge

Young man displaying his wares
Bloor Street, Toronto

Gila enjoying Paris

Gila's room mates at the youth hostel. Toronto, March 2008

A new direction

When I got home I got down on my knees and opened the little prayer book at the Night prayer, which concluded with:

*Let what I have done today be sown for an eternal harvest.*

## 24 December 2006

I enjoy singing on the radio. I had the privilege of being the breakfast guest on the religious show on BBC Radio Cambridgeshire from 8 –8.30 this morning. It was a mixture of conversation and music. They asked me about my Jewish childhood, *The Little Sisters of Joy* and the meaning of Christmas, to which I replied that Christmas wasn't just for 24th December, but that the birth of Christ could happen anywhere, any day and any time.

I sang them the song of the angels, as Jews sing it all over the world on the eve of the Sabbath. At the end, they played one of my favourite pieces of music, the aria *Ombra Mai Fu* by Handel from his opera *Xerxes.* This Persian king walking in his garden under the plane tree reminds me of Nehemiah's mission, in which he asked the Persian king to release him from his duties so that he could return to Palestine and rebuild the Temple. It is a very poignant piece and also reminds me of my own mission of Peace and Reconciliation.

The interview must have gone okay because Marisa sent me an email to say that her husband had woken her up to remind her about it and that I had done a good job, especially in the part about Christmas. She also said that radio suited my voice! A lovely way to end the year!

## 7 January 2007

Yesterday's Epiphany is one of my favourite Feasts. Towards the end of last year, I received a charming letter from a lady in St Leonard's Church. She was confirming an invitation from their Vicar, whom I had met in the University Library, to preach in their ancient church in Catworth in Huntingdonshire, and we chose this Feast.

A Catholic friend drove me all the way down there and when I was installed behind the choir, Stuart, the Vicar, announced that I was probably the first Catholic to preach there since the Reformation! The choir sang sweetly, I preached about the light coming out of the darkness, with reference to the Holocaust and finally sang *Eli, Eli*.

We were given a very good supper afterwards and shown the greatest courtesy and my friend drove me home through the dark of the East Anglian countryside.

## 11 January 2007

Risa Domb died today. Fortunately a close friend told me; otherwise I would have been completely devastated. Risa was a wonderful teacher and the Founder-Director of Cambridge University's Centre for Modern Hebrew Studies, which started in 1993. She moved *'between two landscapes'* in the UK and Israel, where she was born in the town of Netanya.

She was a wonderful friend to me through good times and bad. After my breakdown in 1991, she came to Newton Road and suggested to me that I save myself some stress and finish the degree with just the Hebrew and not the Arabic too. She once said that she felt very close to me and she was very supportive of *The Little Sisters of Joy*. *'There will be hostility, but you've got to go on with it,'* she said, and *'Never be afraid of confrontation to get to resolution.'* It was Risa who insisted that we must be a community of Reconciliation as well as Peace.

In January 1999 before I met Cardinal Lustiger I wrote him a letter, composing it through the night at the Convent of The Sisters of Adoration in Paris. In the morning, I handed it in to a young lady in Notre Dame. When I turned round there was Risa on a visit with her husband – we hugged each other for a long time and I took it as a sign of great grace.

**12 January 2007**

**Saint Marguerite Bourgeoys**

I was praying last night with my French prayer book and asking that I would be able to raise the full amount required by the Canadian government to start the emigration process. (I have already managed to raise most of it.) I turned to the back of the book, only to discover that today is the Feast day of the only Canadian woman Saint. I was reading the brief details of her life when the phone rang and it was my friend to say she was sending the money. Strange how I am only discovering Saint Marguerite in the wake of Risa's death.

Saint Marguerite was born in 1620 in Troyes in France, went as a missionary to Canada and educated French and Indian children, building the first school in Montreal. She founded the Congregation of Notre Dame and died on 12 January 1700. She was canonised by John Paul II in 1982.

**4 February 2007**

**New Year for Trees again**

Last night, Kitty Stidworthy very kindly offered her beautiful home in Newnham for a celebration of our eighth anniversary. Ten Friends and Associates were present, including Françoise Barber, who has so lovingly translated the Rule of Life into French. We celebrated with shared food and drink. Evita, who works in the Victoria café with Alexia, made a beautiful floral decoration.

I gave a brief overview of what has happened in the last year and the plans for Canada. I will be making another trip next month. Kitty read from her translations of Russian poems and I sang. Everyone sang spontaneously in Russian at the end!

Kitty and I later agreed that there was a special grace working throughout the evening. I discovered that she is the only person I know who has been to St Étienne-du-Grès, the village in which the *Sisters of Pomeyrol* live in Provence and where, under God's grace, the concept of community started.

**7 February 2007**

On 5 February, I got my new passport. At 4.30 pm, I caught the Edinburgh train from Peterborough to London and took a taxi to my sister-in-law Roberta's flat in St John's Wood. We enjoyed our time together and I spent a comfortable night. In the morning she asked if I would like a leather shoulder bag which had belonged to Alan, her late partner. He had used it for his passport and documents when travelling all over the world. I was very touched and burst into tears.

At 8 am, we took a cab to Grosvenor Square and the Canadian

High Commission. We walked round the corner to the Immigration Department. As we walked up the steps, the door opened; the Porter ushered us in and there were only a few other people there.

I explained my business and he asked if I had any questions – no, I replied. Upstairs, alone with the porter, I said a Hail Mary and crossed myself and put the brown sealed envelope with the forms and bank draft into a rather nondescript white post box. The porter said he hadn't seen anyone pray there before. All in all it was quite ceremonial and, downstairs again, Roberta said that going there was something to share. I was and am deeply grateful to her.

**1 March 2007**

I am in my flat, the Haven, and am facing a beautiful sunset. Golden clouds in a blue sky. Tomorrow, on the 14.30 plane, I head westwards, flying Globespan to Canada.

Yesterday I was in the Graduate Centre, waiting for Alexia. I sat on the third floor, looking out on to that magnificent view over the River Cam. I suddenly felt a deep feeling, not yet experienced in all these adventurous years: a promise, a light, an expanse in my heart and a beauty that had not yet existed. Someone had said to me the day before, '*A new life beckoning*'.

The One beckoning is Christ, Our Lord, and He is the Light.

**26 March 2007**

I arrived in Toronto at midnight on the 2 March, after sitting in a snowstorm for three hours in Montreal airport. Immobile on the tarmac, I nonetheless felt I had *come home*. Peering out of the window, I saw three brightly coloured planes gliding towards me in a kind of dance.

The welcome at Stella Maris, the community of Sisters and laywomen in which I stayed throughout, has been fulsome. We are from Africa, Canada, El Salvador, Austria and South Korea, and my Jewish flavour added to the mix. We are living in a beautiful house near Bloor and Spadina, where we eat and pray together, taking turns to do the cooking and rejoicing in our graces at mealtimes.

These meals are lively; from time to time Sister Isobel shares the Scriptures with us, drawing from the modern Rabbinical commentaries she is well versed in. Sister Ursula, also from Africa, regales us with a rendering of *O Canada*, (she is becoming a citizen). She is managing the house beautifully and is keeping the show on the road.

The weather has been cold, but I brought the right clothes and I am enjoying the freshness of it all. Most days have been spent walking around the local neighbourhood, called The *'Annexe'*, because it is 'annexed' to the downtown area. Everything is to hand; the Jewish Community Centre with its swimming pool, study classes and café, Susan's second-hand bookshop, shops of every kind, the subway station and Spadina trams, running the length of Spadina Avenue down to King Street.

The local library is next to the Native Canadian Centre on Spadina Road. Between the two, down a little path, is a block of apartments where a group of Native Canadian women live. I have seen them occasionally and I have been to their centre once or twice; they have a ravishing gift shop where they sell things from different Native Canadian traditions.

Hidden behind the local library is a street that opens out into a kind of square. Walking along it one day, I passed a brown apartment block of about ten storeys, where a man was walking in the garden. He turned out to be the caretaker, and said they didn't advertise but there were usually apartments available. Maybe I have found somewhere to live? It's a fascinating community of artists, poets and musicians, amongst others.

It was important to get the Church's blessing, but I hadn't expected to meet the new Archbishop! His name is Archbishop Thomas Collins; he formerly worked in Alberta and had only been in his post for a month when I arrived. During a short meeting with him, he said he was very happy for me to 'plant' myself in Toronto and to let him know when I arrive for good. He knows Hebrew, studied Theology at Ratisbonne (where Maryvonne was) and is interested especially in the hospitality dimension of *The Little Sisters of Joy*.

I am leaving Toronto in two days' time with a very warm feeling in my heart, both for the city and for the people. Who knows what the future holds?

**26 April 2007**

I've got a blog! Alexia and I went to a friend's flat to use her computer and she set me up with my own blog! It was a strange feeling, but I took courage in both hands and wrote on the first Post:

*My name is Sister Gila and you are my global family*

**8 July 2007**

Alexia has finished her Master's in Business and is going back to France soon. I hired a car and we have been to the countryside in Suffolk, where today Anthony, my priest friend with the wonderful voice, gave a little concert with some of his friends. The setting was the old Catholic church in Kirtling and Alexia took a lot photos, including some of the performers. Anthony sang some lovely operatic arias. Afterwards we had a picnic in a nearby field!

## 16 July 2007

I woke up yesterday morning around eight o'clock and had the strong feeling that I should go and visit Peggy, David's mother. I hadn't been able to go for a while. A nurse was waiting in the corridor outside her room. When I went in I could see that she was peaceful, but dying. The nurse asked me if I could handle it and I said I could and that I wanted to be alone with her for a while.

I reflected a little about her early life from what I could remember. She had been born in India, while her father was serving in the British Army. She told me once that she went to school on a horse, with the Himalayas as a backdrop. She believed in God as a child and into her youth; her father had decided to become an Anglican priest, but he lost his faith and she was teased at school about it. Somewhere along the way, her faith became shaky, too, but when she came to live in Cambridge and was walking past the big Catholic Church, she would feel something '*drawing her in*' but never quite had the courage to enter.

I sat and prayed quietly and then I had an idea. I told the nurse that I had to go and get something and quietly slipped down the stairs and out the front door. My memory had served me well; at the bottom of the street there was a brand new farm shop. I went in and told the assistants that I was going to give someone the last rites and did they have a brand new bottle of olive oil?

They were only too happy to sell me one and the young man syphoned off a small amount into an empty coke bottle. He said I could come back for the rest later.

I returned to the home and slipped back up to Peggy's room. She still looked very peaceful. I took some oil between my fingers and made the sign of the cross on her forehead. I said a prayer and stayed with her for a while.

She died at two o'clock today on the Feast of Our Lady of Mount Carmel. I have already adopted a Carmelite as one of the patron saints of *The Little Sisters of Joy* and now surely we have another one.

## 22 July 2007

I took Alexia to Thompson's Lane Synagogue yesterday. As we were crossing Magdalene Bridge, we overtook Rabbi Reuven and three of his children, who looked delightful. The service was moving and Alexia was intrigued by the rocking back and forth, which accompanied the men's prayers. She has invited me to come to France in September to visit her family.

## 27 July 2007

Sat my last Maryvale exam in London today. Must admit it was a great relief.

## 2 August 2007

A really special thing happened today. I was walking up Trinity Street, opposite the craft market area, when I heard a foreign language I was familiar with. I turned round and yes, the young man was speaking Hebrew! We exchanged a few phrases – he was with a group – and I explained I was on my way to a special shop to buy some kosher wine and challah bread for the Sabbath tomorrow. What about celebrating together?

We agreed that the whole group, about twenty in total, and their leader, would meet me tomorrow at 5 pm in the craft market area. The young man could say the blessings, we would share the bread and I could bring my guitar.

## 3 August 2007

We had a wonderful celebration. We all gathered and celebrated Shabbat. My young friend donned a *kippah*, a prayer hat, and said the blessings over the wine and bread. All the students were happy that I brought my guitar because they liked to sing – we danced a little, too. The song they liked best was *Hinay Ma Tov*, Psalm 133, '*Behold how good and pleasant a tribe of brothers together*', that I had sung in the concert in Clare college.

I had told them I was a Christian and they were interested in the background to my life. I had brought a copy of my book, *The Moving Swan,* and their leader said she would take it to Israel and 'tell my story'.

It was only as I was leaving that I spotted the group of silver birch trees in the corner.

## 5 August 2007

It was baking hot today. I was on the bus coming from town when something made me jump off the bus at Chesterton Road – I thought I would like to have a drink in the Arundel House Hotel. As I stepped off the bus, a man in his forties was right across my path. We exchanged a few words (he had a transatlantic accent) and he turned out to be from Toronto and a PhD student in Hebrew and the Septuagint in the Faculty of Divinity!

We just kept on walking while my story unfolded. When we came to the Old Spring we went in and had a couple of beers. He has many contacts and has given me the name of a rather charismatic retired bishop, who is a former Auxiliary Bishop of Toronto. He spoke of all the Catholic University Colleges and said it was an exciting time to be a Catholic in Toronto right now.

I also discovered that his friend, Francis from Toronto, is coming to Cambridge to give an exhibition of his '*wilderness*' paintings at Michaelhouse.

### 8 August 2007

I have booked my Eurostar to Paris for the 18–27 September. But first I have been invited by a Hungarian friend, Tunde, to spend eight days in her home town in Hungary. Apparently we will divide our time between Gyöngyös, in the Matra Hills, and Budapest, the capital. We met here in the Engineering Faculty, where she was working in the cafeteria, and I have been popping in to see her from time to time and chatting about *The Little Sisters of Joy*. She is interested in joining me.

### 7 September 2007

I have been back from Hungary for three days. When I stepped off the plane in Hungary ten days ago, I experienced an intense heat which was completely new for me. Tünde was there to meet me and drove me into the centre of Budapest, where we visited the Great Synagogue and prayed the *Kaddish*, the Mourner's Prayer, for Cardinal Lustiger, who has just died, and for some of Tünde's relatives who had lost their lives quite tragically. The synagogue was large and impressive, as were many of the buildings in the city. I enjoyed listening to the language and there seemed a lot of young people around.

Tünde's home town is forty-five minutes' drive from Budapest, through the Matra Hills, and we bowled along in her little car. We arrived late at night and she told me about her elderly aunt, who lived next door. When I woke up in the morning, I was surrounded by apricot trees! Somehow, through the language barrier, Tünde's aunt and I managed to communicate and I would often see her hanging out her washing or climbing up the ladder to the fruit trees in her neighbouring garden to pick the best fruit. Her legs were quite wobbly and sometimes I would be able to help her.

There was a little grocery store on the corner of the street where I was despatched to buy the groceries so that the locals could get to know me. It gave me a chance to have a look round the neighbourhood and one day Tünde lent me her bicycle to go into the post office – I took the chance to use the Internet and have some very delicious ice cream.

Tünde told me that the Synagogue building still existed and she took me there in her little car. The Jewish community had only left in about 1965 and there is still Hebrew writing at the entrance to the former prayer hall, although the building has now become a furniture store.

We did other lovely things, like going to Eger for the thermal baths. On a visit to Budapest, we visited the National Museum and I danced high above the Danube to the sound of the gipsy violins. I decided I would like to spend an extra few days in the capital and I travelled home from there.

### 18 September 2007

I got myself down to the Eurostar with my guitar and waited on the platform. There was a group of American ladies on their way to the continent. I got talking to one of them and she told me that she was also a child of the 60s and would I play them something on the train?

Once inside, I took up the guitar and put my foot up on the seat. Just as I struck the first chord, the train moved off: it seemed a symbolic moment. The American ladies joined in *Blowing in the Wind* and other favourite songs of the 60s, and we cruised happily to the Gare du Nord.

Alexia was there to meet me and it was a joyful reunion. She drove me to Villecresnes, where I am staying with her and her family for a couple of nights before going to a small hotel near the centre of Paris. Tonight I played and sang for her parents and their neighbours – they joined in! Everyone is very cordial and I feel quite at home.

## 21 September 2007

It has been the Jewish New Year and tonight is *Kol Nidrei,* the eve of the Day of Atonement. I have taken the chance to travel down to Provence, to see *The Sisters of Pomeyrol*. It is the first time I have been here since the tremendous grace and the genesis of *The Little Sisters of Joy* in December 1998. I feel as if I remember every stone and leaf of this Provençal landscape. Tonight, I am accompanying the Sisters to an ecumenical prayer meeting in the old Protestant church in Arles.

## 23 September 2007

The prayer meeting went well the other night and there was some Hebrew singing. I was able to explain the significance of Yom Kippur and the fact that the people at the meeting were in solidarity with the Jews around the world, praying for reconciliation and atonement, too. Afterwards, a lady told me that relations between the Catholics and the Protestants were good in Arles. I went towards the car with the nuns and saw a lighted carousel in the street. Just like the one I had seen in the heart of Paris, near Notre Dame in 1999, just before I met Cardinal Lustiger.

**7 November 2007**

**Graduation Day**

Stayed with a friend last night and arrived today at St Chad's Cathedral in Birmingham in time for Mass. Afterwards we all went downstairs for the robing – Dr Renfrew had measured me up perfectly at home – and it was lovely to see everyone in their finest. There was quite a lot of banter and, after several photos, professional and otherwise, we all went upstairs in a cheerful mood.

I had a long red and black skirt on and, when it came to my turn, I hitched up my skirt and ran up the steps, to be greeted by Lord David Alton MP who beamed at me and said, '*That must have been hard work!*' He presented me with the degree, which is validated by Maynooth University, flanked by Father John on one side and Father Paul, Head of Maryvale Institute, on the other. It was a proud moment.

**12 November 2007 Archive**

After advice from archivists in France and Cambridge, an archive of *The Little Sisters of Joy* has been started. The first box file has been placed with Father John Patrick at Blackfriars, home of the Dominicans. It comprises various documents, such as the Rule and Constitutions, Reverend Polkinghorne's article and the Foundational Statement, along with some photos of people connected to the Project so far.

**2 December 2007, early morning**

My dear little silver birch is growing rapidly, tall and strong with a lovely white bark. A gentle, wise man told me recently that the native Canadians revere this tree and use the bark to make their canoes. This man, who looked like one of those peoples himself with his tanned skin and similar clothes but was actually Caucasian, told me a lot that he knew about the various tribes, and it was evident that he had spent time amongst them. Certainly my tree has a life and a soul, and every day I watch the progress of *The Little Sisters of Joy* through its growth.

**17 February 2008**

A green canoe is wafting its way gently past the window of Henry's Bar, where I have taken refuge after the concert. The couple in it, one woman and one man, are smiling and look happy. Lots of seagulls are flying criss-cross above the river near the large Fellow's Garden of Magdalene College. The great weeping willow looks yellow in the sunlight.

I think that last night's Concert for Peace and Reconciliation, in memory of Risa Domb, was a success. I had prepared myself well with several rehearsals, the last with Vivian Choi in the actual venue, the Lee Hall in Wolfson College. Chinese, like the benefactor of this lovely hall, Vivian is a wonderful professional pianist who lent me her ears and made comments on my performance, both from the musical and from the visual point of view. She suggested I sing 'off the floor' – not on the small stage, as I would be too remote from the audience. Yesterday, the chairs had been put in the wrong position, so I spent an hour re-arranging them in semi-circles, so that I could see and interact with the audience.

I had a curious experience just before the concert began. Marilyn, the conference administrator, had given me a 'green room' in an adjacent house to rest and prepare myself in before the concert and during the interval. In the middle of the room was an oval wooden table. The window to the left as you walked in overlooked the beautiful Chinese and English garden. And something else … from the window on the right side of the garden, you could see the concert hall. As I looked out of the window at about 7.45 pm, I could see the stage and a few people seated in the rows of chairs. I had a sense of calm mystery.

I decided to shut the curtains so that I couldn't see how many people had turned up. Then, at about 7.55, five minutes before it was due to start, I opened the curtains again and reckoned there were about twenty or so people there and said to myself, '*I have an audience*'. When I draped myself in the beautiful red and gold velvet shawl that Pam had given me long ago to walk the short distance to the hall, I felt, for the first time in my life before a performance, utterly calm, without any trace of nerves. As I heard the clock from outside striking eight, I prepared myself to go. As pre-arranged, the Wolfson student knocked on the front door and we made our way together.

**27 February 2008**

**Sanderstead**

I left Cambridge a few days ago to spend the week before flying out to Canada with a friend. Her name is Joy and we met two years ago on a Peace Weekend at Little Gidding. She offered me a place to stay anytime. So, a little while ago, I rang her and said that I needed a little haven between the concert in February and my departure for Toronto, scheduled for 1 March. She agreed immediately and I was struck by her generosity, even at that early stage.

Sanderstead is a place of great beauty. Being in the Greater London area I hadn't expected it. The village is on the top of a hill, surrounded by magnificent trees, and is generally very hilly – a total contrast to Cambridge. My friend's flat is adjacent to the church of All Saints which dates back to the 13th century, with a large Saxon tower. There is a lot of light and the sunsets are magnificent. Two Canadian geese have set up home at the pond; apparently they have been there for quite a while.

## 1 March 2008, late evening

I arrived in Toronto after a very happy journey on British airways. It is not as cold here as I had imagined, although they had a snowstorm last night. Gordon met me at the airport. I have begun to settle into the youth hostel on Church Street, near King, and have two delightful room-mates. I am surrounded by beautiful tall buildings including skyscrapers, and the CN tower is glistening in the dark in its new and vibrant colours. I am reminded of the first time I saw it (when I returned to the city in 2005), but then it was sunrise and I was praying in my little prayer book, '*Help me to build a new life and a new world*'.

Across the street is the Anglican Cathedral of St James; a lovely bell is tolling the half hour at 9.30 pm.

## 7 March 2008

I got on the subway at Sheppard-Yonge in a snowstorm to see Bishop Pearse Lacey. Francis Dvorak, the artist, had finally put us in touch. Father Pearse (as I am to call him) is an artist, too, and had taken lessons from Francis. After I sent him some of my writings on *The Little Sisters of Joy*, he wrote me a beautiful two-page letter by hand, saying how much he would welcome me to Toronto. He included the lines, '*Your Jewish background will be a valuable dimension in the presence of The Little Sisters of Joy in our Diocese.*' It was a wonderful tribute and maybe even something I can show to Immigration.

I nipped into a MacDonald's to avoid the snowstorm on

Sheppard-Yonge. About 10 am, I asked a lady where to find the Bishop's apartment. It was right across the street and I would never have found it on my own. It is an impressive building and beautifully laid out. After speaking to the concierge, I took the lift up to the eighth floor. At the door I took off my large green wellingtons. The door was opened by Rita, Father Pearse's sister. She welcomed me in and we chatted for quite a while, (Father Pearse was in the shower), and I noticed the small coffee table laid for Mass. When Father Pearse joined us, I was taken by surprise – he is a big and jolly man with a round face, who apologised for walking with a cane.

When we were alone, he asked how he could help me, what I needed from him; I replied that I simply needed a friend. At ninety he is still going strong and we both feel that it is through grace that we have been brought together. Father Pearse said Mass for five of us, the other two being neighbours he had known for over fifty years.

Rita made a lovely lunch and Father Pearse regaled us with his experiences of guiding his flock when the enormous changes of Vatican II came in, and how he was amongst the eighty Canadian Bishops who entertained John Paul II at the Convent of the Sisters of St Joseph in the 1980s. His beautiful paintings were all round the walls, along with the handsome portrait of him by Francis Dvorak, but my happiest moment came when, after lunch, he said to me , *This home is your home.*

**8 March 2008**

**Robarts Library**

Snow has been falling since the early morning. After breakfast and phone calls, I headed off in full gear to the subway and landed in St George and the Robarts Library on the university campus. Today is International Women's Day and the few people who were on the street were friendly. One woman told me of the women from the sweatshops in New York who held a protest rally in the 1900s; probably my ancestors, I said. A lady called Doris was ploughing through the snow, looking for the library and it felt good, as I took her arm, to be guiding someone from Toronto to Robarts! The exhibition she was looking for didn't exist and I worried about her as I saw her disappearing out the door about half an hour later. But it was too late to follow her – my stuff and coat were on the third floor.

**11 March 2008, 10 pm**

At 6 pm, I went 'on spec' to my cousin's house in the north of the city, a long subway ride, then a bus. An 'angel' showed me the last part of the way. Tonight, in a snowy landscape of beautiful houses and a cold, clear sky, I knocked at their door for the first time; my cousin's daughter opened it and welcomed me. She and her partner have taken over the family home. After the initial surprise, she made me tea, I played her guitar and she talked to me while practising her harp. I thought the meeting went well and she said she would like to come to see me this Thursday.

**17 March 2008**

My mother would have been 99 today, on St Patrick's Day. To honour her memory, I went to the 8.30 am Mass at the cathedral; it was nice and quiet and Father Missio from the choir school, who had taken an interest in my Project, was celebrating the Mass. His spread-out fingers above the altar were beautiful and reminded me of Psalm 8 which says, *'When I see the heavens, the work of your hands...'*. This is in translation; the actual word in Hebrew means *fingers.*

We have started Holy Week. I have been blessed in that a Religious Sister I met in Walmer Road in the Annexe has lent me her apartment for five days, while she is away. If God really brings me here, with or without a group, Walmer Road is where I would really like to live, in one of the lovely apartment buildings there. I have made another friend in the same block; her name is Yolanda, she is retired and we have arranged to go out for a meal in the Hungarian restaurant round the corner on Bloor.

At 4 pm today I made a friend in the Jewish community. David Novak, a leading light in Jewish Christian relations over here, invited me to meet him in the University. We have been in touch by email and he sent me an article to read. It was on my patron Saint Edith Stein. I made a suitable response (I had differing views on some things) and had a little trepidation about this meeting, but in the end it went well. He was warm and welcoming in what I was trying to do. He even described the different Jewish communities in Toronto in the event I came to live here and signed a copy of his latest book on the Chosen People, which he gave to me as I left.

### 20 March 2008

Just before I went into town, I made a little pilgrimage of a few hundred yards along Walmer Road to where there is a tiny park with some benches. In the middle of the park is the sculpted head of Gwendolyn MacEwan, a poet from the Annexe who died some years ago. I had discovered her on a previous trip and, once again, I was struck by the last two lines of a short poem engraved under the sculpture:

*Under the silver trees we are still dancing, dancing.*

**27 March 2008**

It's four days before leaving and this morning I had a moving talk with one of my room-mates. Born in the north of England, she has worked with animal shelters and is making her own comparative study. She has the feeling that some power is guiding her and moving her around to the right places; what I call 'God' she calls 'instinct'. She is one of the few people to whom I have told of a passage I found in the Bible which has a profound meaning for my current life:

> *I have given you trial by fire,*
>
> *I have given you trial by water,*
>
> *And now I bring you*
>
> *Into a spacious land.*

We agreed it was not about money, but ease and joy and fruitful living.

**20 April 2008**

**A Polish Passover**

Although I had not planned to celebrate it, the first Seder night back in Cambridge was radiant and I have dubbed it '*A Polish Passover*'. Last night, I was at Ania's lovely home, celebrating the Passover with her friend Asha. The table looked glorious and I lit the festival candles from a beautiful candelabra, singing the blessing in Hebrew. The three of us women covered our heads with headscarves in the traditional way. The table was laid with the ritual foods and herrings in dill sauce (a Polish and Jewish delicacy) and glasses of red wine, the crowning glory being the large glass for Elijah the prophet, which takes pride of place at the Passover table.

As our little ceremony unfolded, Ania reflected on how the two traditions, Jewish and Christian, so closely and inextricably interwoven, could have become, over the centuries, so separated in people's minds and hearts. I felt proud of her as she spoke and couldn't help noticing that the little Hebrew prayer book, which I had given to her at the beginning of our friendship, seemed to be gleaming at me from the bookshelf in the corner of the room.

As I sang another melody in Hebrew, Asha said how happy she felt with people of different religions all sitting round the table together.

As is the custom, towards the end of the ceremony we opened the front door for Elijah the prophet, herald of the Messiah. We had just closed it again when there was a ring on the doorbell and there was Father Piotr, the Polish Priest! He is a large, round man in his forties, with shining eyes that I only noticed for the first time when he sat down at table. He had had no idea that he would be participating in a Passover but, in his own inimitable way, he entered into the spirit of it and it was a privilege to have him there. Ania suggested that he might like to drink the wine from Elijah's glass and she gave him a lengthy explanation of it which, I am sure, touched him deeply.

In the end, I stayed the night and I felt *'my cup was overflowing'* as I lay down to sleep. Early next morning, I walked the short distance to St Laurence's Church and attended Mass, on the Fifth Sunday of Eastertide.

**30 April 2008**

**Paris again**

I had lain down to take a rest around 6 pm, having just arrived in Paris by Eurostar. Suddenly I heard the pealing of the bells from the Church of the Immaculate Conception, just down the street from my little Hotel Cosy. I realise they were calling folk to the first Mass of the Ascension, when Jesus is lifted up to heaven, in the sight of His disciples, from the Mount of Olives. It is one of my favourite Feasts and hearing the bells reminded me of the bells in the village, calling me to the Christmas morning Mass, when I was staying in Pomeyrol in 1998.

**1 May 2008**

Alexia came, as planned, to the restaurant Cosy, at 11 am. I had already bought a sprig of muguet, lily of the valley, to present to her and she arrived, carrying a sprig, to present to me! As I was waiting for her, anxiously looking out of the café window, it was touching to see everyone, old and young, carrying the flowers, off to present them to someone they loved. The flowers Alexia brought me had a much more pungent scent than mine, as hers were plucked directly from the woods which surround her home.

It was a beautiful meeting; the town was quiet because of the holiday and we walked arm-in-arm over a bridge near the Avenue du Mande. I think it calmed her a little from the busy life she has at the moment, travelling through France introducing new software for her firm. And studying as well.

Tonight I am having a Chinese meal for the second time in a modest establishment, this time right next door to the Hotel Cosy. It never ceases to amaze me what lovely things are on your doorstep.

**6 May 2008**

**The Opera**

Speaking of lovely things, I had an unexpected experience this morning. After a bumpy ride on the RER, I alighted next to the metro Opera. Passing the glorious Opera House, I wondered whether the auditorium might be open. I was in luck; for eight Euros I was able to enter and see most of the building, including the stage. And the lady at the kiosk said I could sing. Two American ladies were looking at the auditorium from one of the boxes at the side. (I was in one higher up.)When I launched into *Hinay Ma Tov,* the beginning of Psalm 133, the ladies were touched and said they enjoyed my singing very much. I continued with *Plaisir d'Amour,* while a Japanese lady from a box on the other side of the auditorium took my photograph.

I felt light, happy and free. Even more so when I launched into *Nel Cor Piu Non Mi Sento*, a frothy little arietta in Italian that I learned at the beginning of my singing training in Glasgow in 1980. I carried on singing as I walked down the steps of the vestibule of the Paris Opera. I kept going outside as the people sat on the steps enjoying the sunshine of the Place de l'Opera and carried on singing all the way to the Café de la Paix across the street.

**22 June 2008, Ely**

This afternoon, something happened which gave me great pleasure and will hopefully give other people pleasure too. I took my guitar to Ely and made a CD of six religious pieces in St Mary's Church, which nestles beside Ely Cathedral. The inspiration for this came from my friend and fellow musician Sue Gilmurray – her husband Bob is an expert at this and engineered the whole thing, while Sue listened. I wrote three original pieces of music to go with the words of the Magnificat, the Benedictus and a French poem for the Feast of Corpus Christi. The first two were from the Evening and Morning Prayer in English and the third from the French version of the same.

I was particularly happy with the setting of the Benedictus, because the inspiration literally fell upon me when I had just come out of the chapel in the Carmelite monastery in Sclerder, a beautiful spot by the ocean between Looe and Polperro in Cornwall, where I had gone to see my friend, Sister Katrin.

**19 October 2008**

Today we commemorate the martyrdom of the Jesuits who were killed by the Hurons in the 17th century. We remember especially Jean de Brébeuf and Isaac Jogues and their companions. Brébeuf had immersed himself in the Huron way if life and, being a gifted linguist, had made an extensive study of their language. He kept a diary in which he described the deepening of his faith as he sensed he was approaching his inevitable end.

What more fitting day than to reflect on my most recent trip which I made between 29 August and 3 October? It is still fresh in my mind and heart.

This time on my first weekend in Toronto, Eleanor, my goddaughter flew in from Baltimore and spent the first weekend with me. We had lovely long talks and planned to do more when I had trouble with my accommodation. Once again Cousin Gordon came to the rescue and drove me through the snow to the Annexe, where I had the address of a guesthouse. At 9 pm, I rang the bell of a four storey brownstone house in the Annexe and a man in his fifties came to the door. 'D*o you have a spare room*?' I enquired. '*Yes,*' he replied. Looking at him closely I said, '*Are you Jewish*?' '*Yes*,' he replied. And that was Gary. Over the weeks when he got to know me and what I was doing, he said that I could use his home as my permanent address in Toronto. So I have put down some roots over there.

I went to Felicity in the Robarts Library and asked her to find out how I could contact the Chaldean Archbishop. My friend in Cambridge is studying Neo-Aramic, the language of these very ancient Catholic Christians, and asked me to visit him if possible. Before I knew it, I had meeting with His Grace Hanna Zora in their beautiful headquarters on the other side of Toronto. It was a long bus journey but he picked me up at the other end, made me feel quite at ease and asked the cook to make me some yoghurt and eggs with pitta, just as if we were in the Middle East!

Archbishop Zora was deeply interested in my project for Peace and Reconciliation and *The Little Sisters of Joy*, and I felt it was a real meeting of minds and hearts. He even suggested I might find some recruits among the young women in his own flock.

When I visited Fr Pearse again, I discovered that not only did he know Archbishop Zora, but that he was the one in the Church to welcome him to Toronto. What a beautiful web of love! I told Father Pearse what my Chaldean friend had said as I was leaving:

*If you are alone for 100 years, be happy.*

*If you have one with you for 100 years, be happy.*

*If you have lots: THANK GOD!*

Father Pearse smiled and said, '*Isn't that just what you wanted to hear?* '

Casting a shadow over this trip, however, was the fact that my first cousin Ann was very ill. She lived in Drumheller, Alberta, and this place, known as the Badlands and famous for its dinosaurs, was the first place I visited in Canada thirty years ago. Ann sadly died while I was in Toronto; I had already booked a return flight to Calgary and arrived in Drumheller the day after the funeral.

I still had a wonderful opportunity to talk to many people who had known her in different guises. Ann had become an accountant at the age of forty by correspondence course and a lawyer at fifty by going to Calgary University full time. She thought deeply about her Jewish background as she got older and went to evening classes in Calgary, where there is a big Jewish community, to study Hebrew and discover more about her Jewish faith. Soon after she arrived in Canada over 45 years ago, she became a member of the Salvation Army, and was buried in one of their churches.

As is the case after any death, there was a lot of stress in the family. I was staying with her daughter and although it started it out well, the tension between us built up. I was experiencing a bit of culture shock out west as well – Drumheller is quite a small town. I had the idea of phoning the Catholic Cathedral in Calgary and a very nice Indian priest I spoke to on the phone invited me to come and stay for the night on my way back to Toronto with a family from Kerala. It was to be my first experience of Malayalam-speaking Christians and, when I arrived, I was given the honour of opening and closing their prayer meeting. I prayed in Hebrew and the rest was in Malayalam! My hosts were delightful and, by the time I arrived in the airport the next day to return to Toronto, I was feeling much better.

## 15 November 2008

Now I am feeling the after-effects of the trip. I am sitting in one of the small college libraries in Cambridge facing the river. It is a nice bright day and I can hear the happy voices of the people from outside but I feel as if I am barely holding it all together.

## 25 November 2008

The doctors decided that I should come into the psychiatric hospital in Fulbourn near Cambridge, which I am familiar with from previous admissions. I was in Cambridge and trying out my vocation in 1991 when I first had a relapse in my mental health and went into Street Ward. There I met Dr Hymas, the consultant psychiatrist, and we formed a bond which was to last sixteen years. He did me the honour, during that first admission, of coming to hear me with three of his children, when I sang and played on the ward on Christmas Eve.

I have a different psychiatrist this time as I have changed sectors but hopefully it won't be too long before I can go home. Christmas in hospital can be pretty dreary, although I know that my friends will come and visit me.

## 6 January 2009

I woke up this morning on the Feast of the Epiphany and realised that I couldn't emigrate. I will have to work it all out but it makes more sense to base myself here, with my little council flat and all the help the Government is giving me. To say nothing of doctors, dentists and all the other things which keep body and soul together. And maybe it's important to be close to my friends in Europe as well as here.

*My ways are not your ways,* says the Lord. That Canada has tremendous meaning, that much I know.

**February 2009**
Jenny and I met in our usual place this afternoon for tea. She called my whole Canadian experience **'a brave adventure'**. I have the strong feeling that the adventure is not quite over yet.

**Postlude**

The long and winding road that leads to your door… (*Paul Mc-Cartney, Let it Be* album, 1969–70)

My pilgrimage, as I hope you have just read, has taken some amazing twists and turns. In attempting to establish a Religious Community with Pam and others in Benigna's house, I learned a lot about the covenant love between women that is rooted in God and is exemplified in the Old Testament by Naomi and Ruth, and in the New Testament by Mary and Elizabeth.

I hope that through our ministry of hospitality we offered such joy and welcome that bridges were built and people came together in harmony and peace as a result.

This is the ministry I am striving to continue ever since my move over the river to the north side of Cambridge in 2003, in my little flat and in my gatherings in the Regent Hotel and elsewhere.

Since the evolution in 2004 of *The Little Sisters of Joy* into a *Foundation* of Prayer, Peace and Reconciliation, spanning many countries, I feel more free to use the flair and entrepreneurial skills I inherited from my Jewish family, particularly my late father, Joseph. I thank God for the gift of music and the ability to touch people with my singing in Hebrew.

My mystical experiences have sometimes been followed by a period of darkness, but I also thank God that I have realised that He is as much in charge of the darkness as the light and I have always emerged stronger as a result.

If I live as long as my late beloved mother, Dorothea, I have at least another thirty years!